# Art Lab for Kids

For Budding Artists of All Ages

# Art Lab for Kids

## 52 Creative Adventures in Drawing, Painting, Printmaking, Paper, and Mixed Media

Susan Schwake

Photography by Rainer Schwake

QUARRY

Quarto is the authority on a wide range of topics.

Quarto educates, entertains and enriches the lives of our readers—enthusiasts and lovers of hands-on living.

www.QuartoKnows.com

First published in the United States of America by
Quarry Books, an imprint of
Quarto Publishing Group USA Inc.
100 Cummings Center
Suite 406-L
Beverly, Massachusetts 01915-6101
Telephone: (978) 282-9590
Fax: (978) 283-2742
www.QuartoKnows.com
Visit our blogs at www.QuartoKnows.com

**Library of Congress Cataloging-in-Publication Data**

Schwake, Susan.
 Art lab for kids : 52 creative adventures in drawing, painting, printmaking, paper, and mixed
media-for budding artists of all ages / Susan Schwake.
    p. cm.
 Includes index.
 ISBN-13: 978-1-59253-765-5
 ISBN-10: 1-59253-765-0
 ISBN-13: 978-1-61058-211-7 (digital ed.)
 1.  Art--Technique--Juvenile literature.  I. Title. II. Title: 52 creative adventures in drawing, painting, printmaking, paper, and mixed media-for budding artists of all ages. III. Title: Fifty-two creative adventures in drawing, painting, printmaking, paper, and mixed media-for budding artists of all ages.
 N7440.S39 2012
 702.8--dc23

2011041248

CIP

ISBN: 978-1-59253-765-5

Digital edition published in 2012
eISBN: 978-1-61058-211-7

20

Book Layout: *tabula rasa* graphic design
Series design: John Hall Design Group, www.johnhalldesign.com

Printed in China

This book is dedicated with love to my mother,
who always nurtured the artist in me.

# Contents

# Introduction

**THIS BOOK IS A SMATTERING OF LESSONS** I have used over the past twenty years of teaching. They started on the kitchen table with my daughter, Grace, when she was three. Two years and a second baby (Chloe) later, I was convinced that I had to take the art lessons out of the home and share them with others. I opened my little art school in a rented space at a local church. A year passed, and the classes expanded. I moved into a larger studio, then a second location. Finally, it grew up fully into the gallery/studio/school it is today.

Almost every art lesson I taught along the way shared stories about or pictures from contemporary artists. It has been my belief that, through viewing the art of a wide variety of artists, students can identify with a particular movement or singular artist's work. This can reassure young artists of their own work, their own vision.

In our gallery, I curate ten exhibits a year with groups of contemporary artists. The students view the work on a weekly basis, in their classes. Along with the exhibits, books, slides, Internet sites, and posters introduce my students to a broad range of art. However, nothing can replace seeing the actual artwork. I highly recommend visiting a local gallery or museum to see the paintings, drawings, prints, and other artwork in person. It can change your life!

# How to Use This Book and Make Art with Others

**THIS BOOK IS FOR ANYONE** interested in making art with others— or alone. Each Lab is a separate lesson; some are traditionally based; others are not. The units are grouped by medium, and there is some crossover in materials from one Unit to another. The Labs are set up loosely to build skills upon the previous ones; however, you may begin anywhere. Each Lab is a stand-alone project.

In this Unit, I outline what you will need to set up a studio. The list is comprehensive, but you do not need much to get started. I also provide basic steps for using the materials that appear in many of the Labs.

## Some Important Ideas about Making Art with Others

- Each person's work should be wholly his or her own. Don't work on someone else's art. Use thoughtful language when working with others. For example, "Tell me about your painting" works better than "What is that?"
- Always use the best materials that you can lay your hands on for each art-making session. Paper weight makes a big difference in the outcome of a watercolor painting, but you can use recycled flat cardboard with gesso as a primer for acrylic painting.
- Don't worry about wrecking a new paper or canvas. These items can be reused—torn up for collage, primed over with gesso, or printed over.
- Promote fearlessness.
- Embrace individual style. Respect each other's differences.

These Labs are jumping-off points. Explore them with the Go Further suggestions. Try out your own ideas. Have fun! The most important lessons in art are the ones that you discover about yourself in the process. Be brave, experiment, and fear no art!

## Setting the Stage for Creativity

This Unit will prepare you for making art with children and keeping things comfortable and under control in your space, no matter the size of the room. Some of you will work on a student's desktop; others, at your kitchen table. These preparations will help make artmaking comfortable for everyone. Setting up a workspace for creating art can be daunting. These lists and tips can make it easier, whether you are working at home or in the classroom.

## The Master List

A creative place for making art is best fashioned in a comfortable environment, a place free from worry about making a mess. Making art can be stressful for some people—many think it means making a mess or creating havoc. Worry no more! As with so many things in life, preparation is the key to success, and a deeper understanding of a situation is a powerful tool.

The following is a list of items, from simple furnishings to basic materials, to help you build your artmaking space. Collecting these supplies over time is the easiest and most cost-effective way to gather them; however, you might already have many of these items. Keep them in labeled boxes on shelves for easy storage.

1. Natural light or good overhead lighting. Task lighting, such as a clip-on lamp on a desk or table, is useful in smaller group situations.
2. A sturdy table with chairs set at the appropriate height for the student. The height of the table should be approximately at the student's waist, and, when seated, the student's feet should be on the floor.
3. A plastic table covering to protect the surface. Secure it with strong tape to keep it from slipping around.
4. A nearby water source. The best situation is a sink in the room, but buckets of water can work well, with some empty buckets available for dumping dirty water. A plastic tarp or tablecloth under the buckets helps protect the floor.
5. Small plastic containers—round and rectangular, small and large—for holding water.
6. Newspapers, good for just about everything in the mess-control business.
7. Boxes, totes, or shelves for holding supplies. Label them to make finding things easier.
8. Plexiglas or Perspex sheets, about 8" x 10" (20 x 25 cm) in size, one for each student, to use as a palette for painting, printmaking, and drawing. They last forever and are easy to clean.
9. Wax paper and aluminum foil.

10. Fiberboard or Masonite for holding paper securely for drawing or painting.
11. Rolls of clear tape, masking tape, and duct tape.
12. Smocks for protecting the artist. Large men's shirts work well for this, as do old T-shirts.
13. Paper of all sorts: 24-lb. copy paper, 80-lb. sketching paper, 90- or 140-lb. watercolor paper, heavy cardstock, and a collection of fancy colored papers of your choice.
14. Markers of all colors and thicknesses, as well as black permanent markers, crayons, oil pastels, soft pastels, pencils in a variety of hardness, vine charcoal, colored pencils, kneaded erasers, white plastic erasers, and pencil sharpeners.
15. Watercolor pan paints, acrylic paints (both liquid and heavy bodied), tempera paint, gouache, and India ink.

## Making a Good Still-Life Composition

- Choose everyday items that are familiar to you. Don't overlook the simple.
- Vary the height of your objects; for example, try tall bottles with short bowls.
- Vary your textures; include shiny, matte, bumpy, and irregular surfaces.

16. Water-based printmaking ink in black and colors.
17. Brayers for printmaking and mixed-media work.
18. Soft-haired brushes for watercolor and ink and nylon or bristle brushes for acrylic, in a variety of sizes and shapes.
19. Recycled items, including magazines, greeting cards, candy wrappers, old letters, graph paper, colored wrapping paper, maps, old photographs, discarded artwork, discarded books, stickers, stamp pads, balls of string and yarn, embroidery floss, embroidery hoops, small fabric scraps, buttons, textile trims, carded wool, old mats and frames, and poly-foam filling.
20. Found objects for printing or texturing paper; these can include corks, wooden blocks, small sponges, metal washers, corrugated cardboard, lace, craft sticks, pencils with erasers, cookie cutters, straws, plastic toys, tiny cars, cardboard tubes, assorted hardware items, Styrofoam, buttons, and any other items with an interesting shape. Plastic texture plates are available from art suppliers both online and in stores.

21. Adhesives, such as white glue, clear glue, tacky glue, glue sticks, E6000 extra-strong glue, and wood glue, as well as a hot glue gun with glue melt sticks.

22. Canvas boards, canvas paper, stretched canvas, found wood, smooth birch plywood, and fiberboard or Masonite. All should be primed for painting with an acrylic gesso.

23. Kitchen supplies, such as liquid soap, plastic bowls, wooden spoons, sponges, scrub brushes, drinking straws, old cookie sheets, paper towels, rags, clean recycled foam trays from the grocery store, butcher paper, and plastic cutlery.

24. Office supplies, including rulers, stapler, paper clips, bulldog clips, push pins, rubber stamps, and rubber bands.

25. Hardware supplies: hammer, screwdriver, nails, screws, tape measure, metal washers, sandpaper of varying grit, paint-can openers, and foam brushes.

26. A cardboard portfolio to keep work together, or an old magazine rack, a deep drawer or shelf.

27. A display area for finished work; this can be a cork board, a string with clips, or wall space.

## Setting Up an Area for Drawing

Most drawing lessons require little setup and cleanup, and, with the exception of India ink, there is little to spill. Keep India ink in small refillable bottles or shallow containers, and always work on newspaper to protect surfaces from the ink.

When using soft pastels or charcoal, have a damp paper towel nearby to keep your fingers clean.

Make drawing boards to use as a drawing surface (if you are drawing outside or without a table) from pieces of Masonite or thick foamcore. Masking tape or bulldog clips keep paper securely affixed.

Spray fixatives for charcoal and soft pastel should be used only by an adult and applied only outside. To prevent spatters, hold the can at arm's length, and spray with a sweeping motion across the paper.

## Setting Up an Area for Painting

Setting up your workspace makes creating much simpler; when everything is in order, it's easier to focus on painting.

Protect the table with butcher paper, a plastic tablecloth, or newspaper and the floor (if necessary) with a reusable tarp or tablecloth.

Place a folded sheet of newspaper on the right side of your paper if you are right-handed and on the left if you are left-handed. This is where you put your water container, brushes, and Plexiglas paint palette. An extra piece of paper folded in half again is good for wiping off water or excess paint. Set it up this way and you will avoid most accidents.

For acrylic paints, dispense coin-size amounts, add retarder to slow down the drying time, and mix paints with palette knives for easy cleanup. For gouache, a shallow-welled palette for holding small amounts of water and paint works well. Slip a piece of white scrap paper under the edge of your palette for testing colors. When finished with an acrylic painting, you can protect the work by brushing an acrylic varnish over it evenly, or you can spray the work outdoors with a clear-coat finish under adult supervision.

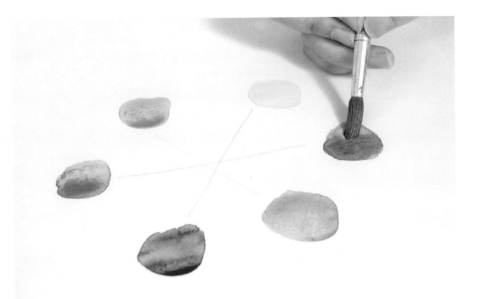

## MAKE A SIMPLE COLOR WHEEL FOR YOUR STUDIO

A color wheel is a helpful tool for choosing colors. You can create a variety of effects by combining colors in different ways. Colors that sit next to each other on the color wheel are called analogous colors. When combined, their effect is harmonious. Complementary colors sit opposite one another on the color wheel and have a strong contrast—for example, orange and blue, purple and yellow, and red and green. Combining complementary colors makes your artwork pop! Throughout this book, you will explore the effects created by using these colors in different combinations.

Use watercolor or acrylic on paper or board to make your color wheel. Think of the wheel as a clock. Paint a spot of red at 12:00, a spot of yellow at 4:00, and a spot of blue at 8:00. Then add a spot of orange at 2:00, a spot of green at 6:00, and a spot of purple at 10:00. This will show you the basic color wheel with the complementary colors.

## Setting Up an Area for Printmaking

Start your printmaking experience by grabbing a stack of newspaper. Open up five sheets to cover your work area. Layering it is best, up to ten sheets, so you can pull away the inky ones and always have a fresh one underneath as you go. Have a shallow rectangular container of water handy to wash the brayers off when changing colors during the process. Have your clean printing paper in a stack nearby but not on your work surface. Number them in pencil in edition form, as instructed below, and sign them. Have a square of damp paper towel near your water container to wipe off your fingers if they get too inky.

Use the Plexiglas palette (or polystyrene plate or tray) for your ink station and a second piece for monotypes. When inking, roll the ink away from you slowly, in line with the width of your brayer and the length of your Plexiglas, or less. Pull the brayer back toward you and continue to roll until the ink is smooth. You can also use foam trays for the ink. Now you are ready to print!

### PREPARING PRINTING PAPERS IN AN EDITION

Printmakers sign their prints by edition. Monotypes are generally one final print, or one plus a second, fainter "ghost print," from one printing plate. Our foam-plate printing plates can make multiple prints, as does the silk-screen process. To prepare the printing paper ahead of time, you can sign the print at the bottom right, put the title in the middle of the page, to the left of your signature; place number of the individual print over the total number of prints in the edition (as if it were a fraction) at the far left.

### GELATIN PRINTING

To make a gelatin plate, start the day before, to allow the gelatin to set up overnight.

Use an unflavored gelatin. Small baking tins are a good choice for molds. The mold can be any size you want, but choose one that will fit the size of your finished artwork: if you're not sure, start with a pan approximately 8" x 10" (20 x 25 cm) in size.

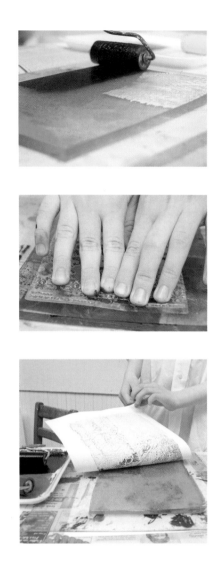

Your gelatin plate should end up being about half an inch (1.3 cm) thick. To determine the amount of gelatin needed, measure the amount of cold water required to fill the mold to half an inch (1.3 cm). You'll need two tablespoons (14 g) of gelatin for every cup of water. Line the tin with plastic wrap, being sure to wrap it over the edges; you'll use the wrap to remove the gelatin when it's set.

To make the gelatin:
- Measure the appropriate amount of cold water in a saucepan. Add the gelatin and stir well to dissolve it completely, and then bring to a boil, stirring all the while.
- Allow it to cool, and then pour the mixture into the prepared mold. Place the mold in a level spot of your refrigerator overnight.
- To remove, gently pull the gelatin out of the mold and place it on the Plexiglas. You can store the gelatin, covered, in the refrigerator for up to a week.

Objects you can print from include corks, wooden blocks, small sponges, metal washers, corrugated cardboard, lace, craft sticks, pencils with erasers, cookie cutters, straws, plastic toys, tiny cars, cardboard tubes, assorted hardware items, Styrofoam, shells, seed pods, old toothbrushes, buttons, and any other items with an interesting shape.

Fruits and vegetables can also be used. Try lemons, onions, lettuce leaves, radishes, mushrooms, celery, broccoli florets (cut in half from the top down), carrots, peppers, and apples or pears (cut in half lengthwise and crosswise for different looks). To cut, use a sharp knife, and cut straight. Blot produce on paper towels to absorb excess juice. A fork stuck into large fruits or vegetables as a handle is helpful for little hands or slippery produce. The produce can be washed off and wrapped and stored in the refrigerator for a week for reuse.

Texture plates are flat plates with a raised pattern and are used to make rubbings. To create a rubbing, place the plate under a piece of paper and rub over the top with a crayon or oil pastel. Texture plates can be purchased from most art suppliers. They sometimes lurk in the preschool or clay sections of catalogs. I have had the same six plates for twenty years and use them almost weekly for one thing or another. They can be replaced with found objects, such as sneaker or flip flop soles, coins, combs, leaves, ferns, lace, corrugated cardboard, or anything else that will create an imprint.

## Paper and Mixed Media

Paper, from junk mail to beautiful handmade papers, can be collected from many sources. For mixed media, consider using old letters, stamps, wrappers, greeting cards, ticket stubs, old books, dictionaries, wallpaper sample books, graph paper, ledger paper, gift wrapping, and cardboard from cereal boxes. Keep a box for your papers and a small envelope for tiny pieces too beautiful to throw away.

### GLUING, TEARING, AND CUTTING PAPER

To keep your artwork from getting sticky, place a piece of scrap paper under your project when gluing paper pieces onto your artwork.

Tearing paper produces a different look from cutting paper. Torn paper gives an organic look, with soft edges; cut paper is sharp and hard-edged.

Paper has a grain just like the wood it's made from. Tearing with the grain is easiest to control. Try this with newspaper to experiment! Tearing across the grain is more difficult. With a colored or printed paper, pulling the paper from the top to the bottom with your right hand leaves the left side of the paper with a white border. Sometimes that white edge or border is perfect for a special outlined look. Keep your fingers pinched close together for the most controlled tearing.

When tearing thick, handmade paper, first draw a line with a wet brush along the tear line, then pull the paper apart.

Cutting paper always gives a crisp edge. If your paper is large, you might want to cut it down before making your detail cuts. Trying to cut a small piece out of the middle of a large piece of paper is challenging. Cut in, to get to it, and then remove the excess around it.

# Drawing

**DRAWING IS A FOUNDATION SKILL FOR ALL ART.** It can excite or intimidate students, depending on where they are on their artistic journey. This Unit will allow students to explore drawing in ways beyond the pencil and paper. Each Lab encourages fearless markmaking and thoughtful line and volume work. Some Labs incorporate a brush and ink or bright watercolors; others use more traditional media. When practicing drawing, many people find the eraser to be their best friend and their worst enemy. For many years, I didn't have erasers readily available for my students, because some spent more time erasing lines than drawing them. I found that, through the use of different media, many students found success, where the pencil and eraser had failed them before. It has been my desire to encourage every student through unconventional methods, endless exploration, and allowing chance to be a viable element in their drawing. Remember, this should be fun! Keep the fun part in mind when embarking on any of these Labs—experience is the focus—not perfection.

UNIT

2

# Contour Drawings

- drawing paper
- permanent black marker, thin or thick point
- soft pencil
- charcoal
- still life made up of simple objects, such as fruit, bottles, bowls, vases, and boxes

**Think First:** Contour drawing is one way to begin any two-dimensional artwork. Arrange your objects so some of them overlap and some have spaces between them. Take a few moments to look at the edges of each of the objects you have placed in your composition. Trace your finger around them in the air to get a feel for their edges. Starting an artwork with a good contour drawing can be very helpful!

## Go Further

- Perform this exercise in your sketchbook each day for a month, using different objects
- Make a "blind contour" drawing by looking at the objects only, not the paper, while you are drawing. This is a great way to improve your ability to "see" the object and train your hand with your eye.

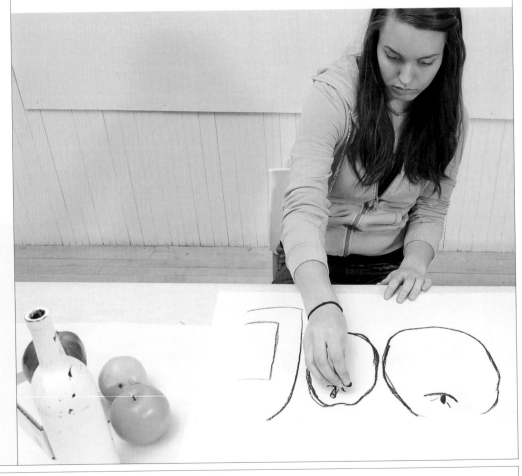

# Let's Go!

***Fig. 1:*** *Follow the edges with your eye to draw them.*

1. After studying the edges of the objects, begin drawing them with the permanent marker, from one side of the composition to the other. Some people like to work from the background to the front. Try both ways to find your favorite (fig. 1).

2. Remember to eliminate all of the extras—just outline the objects.

***Fig. 2:*** *Leave out details and draw just the outline.*

3. Continue to draw all of the objects until they are all sketched in (fig. 2).

4. Draw the same still life with the soft pencil and then with the charcoal (fig. 3).

***Fig. 3:*** *Try the same drawing with charcoal.*

5. Enjoy the process of getting to know your composition through contour drawing with three different materials. You can finish off your artwork with color if you desire.

## Meet the Artist: Rose Sielian Theriault

Rose Theriault, an artist from New Hampshire, has taught high school art for more than thirty years. She works in a variety of media and loves still life drawing and etching. *Pears Squared* is an etching showing the essence of contour drawing. Rose uses this technique often in her bold and beautiful work.

*Pears Squared* by Rose Sielian Theriault

# Large-Scale Ink Drawings

## Materials

- large piece of drawing or watercolor paper
- black ink
- medium-size watercolor brush
- assorted soft pastels or pan watercolor
- container of water
- paper towels
- newspaper
- still life composed of bottles and fruit sitting on a cloth or large piece of paper

*Choose what to draw after setting up your still life.*

**Think First:** Arrange the still life in front of your working area. You want to be able to see all of it but still have space for your drawing paper. Make sure the objects are not too far apart from one another—try a few different arrangements until you are happy with it. Have a seat in front of your paper and still life and decide what you would like to include in your artwork. Remember, the paper is large and you will be making the objects larger than life-size, so think about their placement.

# Let's Go!

Fig. 1: Begin with the objects in the back first, then work your way to the front.

1. After thinking about what parts of the still life you are going to draw, begin with the objects farthest away from you (fig. 1).
2. Using the ink and the brush, without drawing first with a pencil, might seem scary to begin with, but be brave and make your marks boldly and large!

## Meet the Artist: Ernst Kirchner

Ernst Kirchner has a strong distinctive style and often uses ink in his drawings and paintings. He helped found the Brücke artists association in 1905. He enjoyed capturing city street scenes with groups of people. His work *Cocotte with Dog* inspired this Lab. Read more about Ernst Kirchner at www.bruecke-museum .de/englkirchner.htm.

Fig. 2: Be brave!

Fig. 3: Shadows are part of the drawing too; add them with ink or color.

3. Working from the back to the front, draw the still life with the paintbrush, adding all the details that you want to have in black ink. Watch for overlapping objects, and remember to pick up your brush when you come to an overlapping line. Work from one side to the other to avoid smearing your work with your arm (fig. 2).

Fig. 4: Watercolor is a good choice for adding color if you have used a heavier paper.

4. Shadows can be added with ink or with pastel or watercolor (fig. 3).
5. After the work is dry, add soft pastel for color and for shadows, or use some watercolor if you have used watercolor paper.
6. After you add color, you can go back over your black lines with ink to make them crisp (fig. 4).

## Go Further

- Try drawing a portrait of yourself with your family's pet.
- Use only ink, and, instead of color, use shapes or lines to create interest in the shadows, details, and background.

# LAB 3 Scribble Drawings

## Materials

- drawing paper
- pencil
- colored pencils
- optional: watercolors
- scissors
- glue stick for paper
- background papers you have made or bought
- paper towels and newspapers (if using watercolors)

### Go Further

- Collect smaller cut-out scribbles to create a large collage artwork.
- Instead of colored pencils, try watercolors for details, if you use heavy paper.

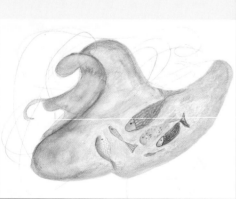

**Think First:** This lesson draws on your ability to let go and scribble. It also engages the part of you that enjoys lying on your back in the grass, looking up at the clouds, and seeing things in the shapes the clouds make. So, relax! Get loose! Imagine things!

*Finished scribble drawing which has been cut out and glued onto a background*

# Let's Go!

*Fig. 1: Keep your drawing loose and loopy.*

*Fig. 2: Outline your objects first with pencil.*

1. Using a pencil, start scribbling in a circular motion, one long line all over your paper (fig. 1).

2. Keep your pencil in contact with the paper at all times, making the scribble in one long motion. Cross often over the lines you have made!

3. Stop when you see there are enough lines on your paper. Do this on at least two pieces of paper.

4. Examine the scribble by holding it up in front of you and turning the paper in all directions. Find objects in the scribble. Outline them with your pencil so they are more apparent (fig. 2). You might not find something in your scribble on your own. If this happens, have a friend take a look at your scribble. She will find something!

5. Using colored pencils, add details and color to the objects you have found (fig. 3).

*Fig. 3: With colored pencil, add details.*

*Fig. 4: Cut out your drawings.*

6. Cut out the objects or add a background, if you prefer (fig. 4).

7. If you cut them out, find a background paper where your scribble drawings could live and glue them onto that paper with a glue stick.

## Meet the Artist: Anne O. Smith

Anne O. Smith is an artist and retired high school art teacher. Her whimsical work includes lots of scribble drawings. A big scribble that she cut out and then redrew became the art piece *Bird Walk*.

*Bird Walk* by Anne O. Smith

# Soft Pastel Drawings

- drawing or pastel paper
- soft pastels
- bouquet of flowers (real flowers are great, but silk ones will work, too)
- a vase
- fixative

*Deciding on a composition*

**Think First:** Set up your still life. Study the flowers. The petals and leaves of each flower have different shapes. Take some time to see each petal and trace it with your finger, first on the flower and then in the air. Is it pointed or rounded? Do the petals have more than one color? Where are they lightest and where are they darkest? Decide if you want to zoom in on a few blooms to fill your page or if you want to draw the entire bouquet. Choosing your composition (what your drawing is going to include and where the objects sit on the paper) now is a good thing.

# Let's Go!

1. Look at your paper and decide which way it should be oriented: horizontally or vertically. Using the pastels, start drawing the vase. If you are zoomed in very close, begin with the largest bloom.

2. Remember that pastels smudge easily, so keep your hand above the paper as you draw. Press lightly—the color flows easily from soft pastels.

3. Continue working out to the edges of your composition with the pastels.

4. Try layering colors, one on top of the other, to get the full range of colors in the petals (fig. 1).

5. Try smudging two colors with your finger to blend them into a new color.

6. Make short marks and long marks for a nice variation in texture (fig. 2).

7. Finish the drawing with a fixative to reduce smudging, as described in Unit 1, page 20.

## Go Further

• Pastels are also a fun medium to use to make portraits and landscapes.

• Try an abstract pastel painting. Start with a shape and repeat the shape, adding lines in between, or a try using pastels for a scribble drawing as in Lab 3!

*Fig. 1:* Layer pastel colors.

*Fig. 2:* Create texture with different kinds of lines.

## Meet the Artist: Mitchell Rosenzweig

Mitchell Rosenzweig is an accomplished artist living in the Greater New York City area. His work ranges from pastels to paintings—often very large—and sculptures. *Wild Sky over Mountains* is one of his beautiful pastel paintings. Find out more about Mitchell's work at mitchellrosenzweig.com.

*Wild Sky over Mountains* by Mitchell Rosenzweig

# LAB 5 Oil Pastel Drawings

## Materials

- drawing-weight paper
- oil pastels
- still life objects (think favorite toy: plush, plastic, wooden, doll)
- small box or container to raise up the objects
- cloth to cover the box, if desired

*Study the objects*

**Think First:** Oil pastels are colorful and creamy in texture. If you like the way an oil painting looks, you will love creating your own masterpiece with oil pastels!

Set up a still life with boxes and some simple (shaped) objects. Make your still life personal by adding of one of your favorite objects, such as fruit, bottles, vases, mugs, rocks, shells, a ball, books, or an interesting houseplant. Things that interest you most are always the best subjects. Smaller objects might be more suitable placed on top of the boxes. Overlap some of the items, and consider spotlighting one of your favorites by placing it farther away from the main grouping. Take a few minutes to really study where the objects are in relation to one another.

# Let's Go!

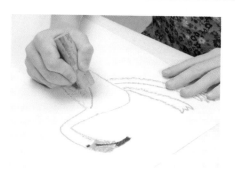

*Fig. 1:* Lightly draw in the contours of the objects.

1. Start by deciding where the objects will be placed on the paper. Think about the size of your paper and the parts of the still life you want to show.

2. Choose your oil pastel colors and lightly draw the contours of the objects (fig. 1).

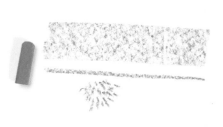

*Fig. 2:* Make short or long lines to fill in.

3. Fill in the objects with short or long lines, depending on whether the objects are smooth or textured or whether you want to follow a particular style (for example, an Impressionist painting) or work in your own style (fig. 2).

4. Use the side of the oil pastel to make broad strokes (fig. 3).

5. Use your finger to blend colors, and try to cover all of the white paper with color, just like a painting.

*Fig. 3:* Make broad strokes using the side of the pastel.

## Go Further

Try this exercise with just one of your favorite stuffed animals, making your artwork very large—just like artist Joe Blajda did. You can even take your composition off the edge of the paper.

## Meet the Artist: Joe Blajda

Joe Blajda is an oil painter and painting instructor. He created a series of paintings about his family's childhood stuffed animals. These oil paintings depict his sibling's animals in a personal and humorous light. This painting is of the artist's own childhood teddy bear. What do you think the bear is thinking?

*Joe's Bear* by Joe Blajda

# 6 Crayon **Scratchboard**

- white cardstock
- crayons
- liquid dish soap
- soft brush
- small plastic container
- India ink
- newspapers
- a small finishing nail for scratching your design

**Think First:** This process allows scribbling and carefree placement of color as well as well-thought-out planning of the final product. I encourage both with my students by giving them two pieces of cardstock: one for scribbling or patterning with color and one for planning out the final look of the piece. For example, a night landscape with fireworks in the sky will need greens or browns at the base of the page for land and colorful fireworks hues in the upper part, the sky. Because of the black ink background, the overall theme is night or darkness, but you can use your imagination and go beyond that prompt. Think caves, deep sea, or even outer space!

## Go Further

- Use a patterned paper and cut out shapes for a greeting card or collage work.
- Cut the cardstock into circles and thread them together with embroidery floss to make a pretty garland.

# Let's Go!

**Fig. 1:** *Press hard with the crayons.*

**Fig. 2:** *Rub the paper to check if it's all waxy.*

1. Select a few colors of crayons that suit your idea.

2. Using a firm hand, fill up the cardstock with crayon, laying down the color in small sections, in patterns, or by scribbling. Press hard with the crayons (fig. 1).

3. Mark the back of the page with an arrow, to show which way is up, and sign your name.

4. When the cardstock is fully covered in color, run your hand over it, to make sure it feels waxy everywhere. If not, add another layer of color to coat (fig. 2).

**Fig. 3:** *Paint over the crayon with the ink mixture.*

**Fig. 4:** *Draw by scratching with a small nail.*

5. Pour a small amount of ink in a small dish, enough to cover the bottom. Add four to six drops of liquid dish soap to the ink and mix it up gently, so you don't create bubbles. The dish soap helps the ink cover the crayon.

6. Using the paint brush, cover the entire sheet with ink until you can't see the base color. Let dry overnight (fig. 3).

7. Using your scratching tool, carefully draw your images into the ink. If you make a line you don't like, you can change your idea, taking it in another direction, or you can simply paint a little ink mixture over the mistake, let it dry, and continue (fig. 4).

## Meet the Artist: Amy Ruppel

Amy Ruppel is an artist from Portland, Oregon. Her portfolio is vast and ranges from illustrations for companies such as Target to fine artworks, as seen in this beautiful black wax painting, *Sly One*. See more of her work at www.amyruppel.com

*Sly One* by Amy Ruppel

# Drawing with an Eraser

- plain newsprint paper, white drawing paper, or gesso-primed canvas
- newspaper
- vine charcoal
- kneaded eraser
- an assortment of white or shiny objects, such as kitchenware, painted bottles, or lightbulbs

### Go Further

- Have a friend sit for you under a bright light and draw his portrait.
- Draw outside during the warmer months with a campfire for a single point of dramatic light.

**Think First:** Set up your still life on a plain cloth or white paper, to show shadows clearly. Cover your work area with newspaper to keep it clean. Charcoal is messy, so have a damp cloth nearby to wipe off your fingertips.

Study the still life. Which parts of it are the lightest, with the highest highlights? Where are the darkest parts? Are there any places so dark that you can't see the outline between objects? Keep these in mind when you are ready to begin.

# Let's Go!

**Fig. 1:** *Cover the paper with charcoal.*

1. Start by covering your paper with charcoal. Holding the charcoal on its side, rub it all over, but leave a border of white paper around the edges (fig. 1).

2. Make a little point with your kneaded eraser and "draw" a faint outline of the objects' contours (fig. 2).

3. Continue drawing in the details with the eraser to show the highest highlight shapes.

**Fig. 2:** *Draw the outline with the point of the eraser.*

**Fig. 3:** *Go back and deepen the darkest areas.*

4. When you have all of the objects and the middle tones of the still life drawn in, go back with the charcoal and deepen the darker areas. A wide range of white to dark is what you are aiming for (fig. 3).

## Meet the Artist: Glen Szegedy

Glen Szegedy is an artist who works with almost all media. His works include giant silk paintings, carvings in alabaster, etchings and woodcuts, and found-object assemblage. He favors charcoal drawing, and this piece, *Desert Frogs,* illustrates the inspired use of an eraser to create a drawing.

*Desert Frogs* by Glen Szegedy

# Drawing Negative Space

- charcoal
- soft pencil
- drawing paper
- objects with interesting profiles
- optional: a box to set the object in, to give it a boundary

### Meet the Artist: Jen Garrido

Of her work, Jen Garrido says, "I construct my paintings and drawings using a delicate balance of choice and process." Her artwork inspired this Lab. See more of her work at jengarrido.com.

**Think First:** This exercise is to help you look at drawing in a different way, by drawing the negative space, or what is not there.

Set up the object with a simple background—white paper or something with a simple pattern, such as stripes. When looking at the space around an object, sometimes the easiest things to find are the simple shapes that the space makes. Look for triangles, circles, and rectangles. Try to focus on those, instead of on the contour or edges of the object. Keep your eye on the space.

*Kissing* by Jen Garrido

# Let's Go!

**Fig. 1:** *Start at the edge of the paper.*

**Fig. 2:** *Keep your eye on the shape of the space.*

**Fig. 3:** *Use the charcoal until the space requires a pencil.*

**Fig. 4:** *Work with two objects.*

1. Set a boundary around the object, either imaginary or with a box. Start at one edge of the paper and draw in toward the object with the side of the charcoal (fig. 1).
2. Keep your mind on the shape of the space (fig. 2).
3. Continue blocking in with the charcoal, until the space becomes too small and you need to use the pencil (fig. 3).
4. Use the combination of the pencil and charcoal to finish your drawing.
5. Practice this with one or two objects in a setting, until you feel comfortable with seeing and drawing the negative space (fig. 4).

## Go Further

- Start with simple objects and move up to objects with a lot of detail, such as a houseplant or vase of flowers.
- Use watercolors instead of drawing materials for this project.

# LAB 9 Oil Pastel Resist

- 12" x 18" (30.5 x 45.5 cm) piece of drawing paper or other heavy paper that accepts water media
- oil pastels
- watercolor pan paints
- watercolor brush
- large water containers
- newspaper
- paper towels
- scrap white paper
- a memory of a place outdoors where you have spent time

**Think First:** Set up your palette as described in Unit 1, page 20. Keep the rest of your materials close at hand.

Think about your memory place in detail, asking yourself the following questions: What time of day was it? What season was it? What was the weather like? What did the sky look like? Was there a lot of sky and a little land or the opposite?

## Meet the Artist: Paul Klee

Paul Klee was part of the Blue Rider group of artists in Germany in the early 1900s. His work is often called child-like and playful. He valued the art of children as well as nature, both of which are apparent in this work. Find out more about Paul Klee and the Blue Rider group online or in your local library. His work, *Growth in an Old Garden,* inspired this lesson.

# Let's Go!

**Fig. 1:** *Draw in the horizon line.*

**Fig. 2:** *Draw in lines and details from back to front.*

**Fig. 3:** *Fill in with watercolor.*

*Colors can mix spontaneously for a soft effect and still have a hard line with the oil pastels.*

Begin with the oil pastels directly. This bold move, eliminating any pencil lines or erasure, is a good exercise in "just doing it."

1. Start with finding and drawing the horizon line—the line where where the sky meets the land or the water (fig. 1).

2. Using the oil pastels, draw in details, from the most distant point in the background to the closest point in the foreground (fig. 2). Vary your line length to show visual texture: short lines for spiked grass or longer lines to show wispy clouds or tall trees. Don't fill in all of the areas with oil pastel. Keep empty spaces between your lines to fill in with watercolor. Large areas such as skies and fields can be mostly paint; details, such as buildings, gardens, and animals, can be mostly oil pastel. White and light-colored pastels make a big impact with dark paint!

3. When you have the entire landscape drawn out with details and texture, you are ready to begin painting. Using a very

wet brush, pick up some paint from the watercolor pan by stroking the brush gently, enough times to pick up a rich amount of color. Stroke the color over the sky first and then work from the back to the front of your landscape. Notice how the oil pastel lines are not covered by the watercolor, even when you paint directly over them! The oil pushes the water away and keeps the lines you have drawn clear of paint (fig. 3).

## Go Further

- Choose a scene outside or an imaginary place in a story and illustrate it with oil pastel resist.
- Use only short lines with the oil pastel to create an Impressionist-style painting.
- Try a nighttime landscape—think camping, fireworks, or cities at night.

A nighttime cityscape

## Materials

- heavyweight drawing paper
- colored pencils
- graphite pencil
- optional: acrylic paint or water-colors and associated brushes
- reference books of animal drawings or photographs

**Think First:** This is a fantasy drawing, so let your imagination run wild. Look through reference books for images of two animals to combine to make your very own new animal. Combine mammal and insect, reptile and crustacean, bird and fish—the sky is the limit.

## Go Further

- Show an entire family of your new animal, complete with male and female and baby animals, or a herd of them!
- Add collage elements to the animal or habitat for texture.

A school of catfish

# Let's Go!

*Fig. 1:* Sketch a few ideas out first.

*Fig. 2:* Draw in a habitat for your animal.

1. Once you have decided on two animals, decide which parts of each animal are going to go where. Try a few thumbnail (small) sketches of your ideas first if you want to narrow down a lot of ideas (fig. 1).

2. With the graphite pencil, draw your new animal in a setting of your choice (fig. 2).

3. Once you are finished with the basic drawing, start adding color and details with the colored pencil (fig. 3).

4. Add watercolor or acrylic, if you wish, or keep the drawing simple with pencil and colored pencil.

## Meet the Artist: Sally Allen

Sally Allen is a mixed-media artist and teacher who often finds curious fantasy animals in her artwork. This painting, *They Danced by the Light of the Moon*, inspired this lesson. More about Sally can be found at www.gentlejourney.net.

*They Danced by the Light of the Moon* by Sally Allen

*Fig. 3:* Add color and details.

# Painting

**MOST PEOPLE HAVE HAD EXPERIENCE WITH PAINTING**
from a young age, usually with tempera paint at a preschool easel, watercolor at the kindergarten art table, or, for a lucky younger few, pudding on their high-chair tray, with happy fingers swirling around! In the classroom, I rarely get an objection from a student when we take out the paints for a session.

I believe the love of painting is something we all have as little children. I also believe that nurturing that love through positive teaching methods can develop a greater skill set within the medium, while retaining a satisfying creative process at the same time. This Unit will guide us through a variety of water-based-media painting experiences, whose end results will be a greater understanding of color theory, value scale, visual texture, composition, techniques, and, most important, an expansion of each person's own emerging style.

UNIT 3

# Painting in the Style of . . .

- primed canvas or board
- pencil
- acrylic paints
- variety of small and large bristle brushes
- image of an artist's work
- water containers
- newspaper and paper towels
- Plexiglas palette

**Think First:** This Lab encourages you to paint through the eyes of a famous artist. Choose a master work that you are drawn to—and love. In this lesson, we are using Georgia O'Keeffe, but any artist you choose will do. Have a good copy of the original work, either from a book or the Internet, to work from.

## Go Further

- Try making the same work on a very large canvas, as Georgia O'Keeffe often did.
- When using another artist's work, try to use the same strokes; choose the same size brushes he or she used to actually "try on" the artist's style.

# Let's Go!

**Fig. 1:** *Sketch the image on the canvas or board.*

**Fig. 2:** *Work from the back to the front of the painting.*

**Fig. 4:** *Add details.*

1. Begin by using a pencil to lightly sketch the contours of the image onto your canvas (fig. 1).
2. Mix the colors for the background and apply them in a thin layer, covering all the white primed canvas (fig. 2).
3. Working from the back to the front, add larger details, using smooth strokes and blending, just as Georgia did.

**Fig. 3:** *Blend the colors carefully.*

4. Mix some more paint and add a thicker layer of paint to the background, blending each color carefully. Continue to the front, adding final details as you go (fig. 3).
5. Pay attention to the subtle color changes, light to dark values, little details, and smooth color transitions that Georgia O'Keeffe used (fig. 4).
6. When you feel you are finished, add a protective coating, as described in Unit 1, page 20.

## Meet the Artist: Georgia O'Keeffe

Georgia O'Keeffe was a beloved American artist. She lived in New York City when she was young and painted many of its buildings at night. Search online to see her well-known painting *The Radiator Building*. Visit www.okeeffemuseum.org to learn more about this artist.

# Tiny Paintings on Wood

- small piece of smooth, gesso-primed wood
- pencil
- acrylic paints
- variety of small bristle brushes
- paper for sketching
- water containers
- newspaper
- paper towels
- idea for the subject of painting: small still life, landscape, abstract, or portrait
- Plexiglas palette

**Think First:** Making a small painting is a fairly quick exercise in getting an idea from your head into a painting. The paintings can be simple or detailed—the choice is up to you, the artist. Decide what you would like to paint from: a still life, photograph, abstract, or portrait. For our example, we used a sunflower as the subject matter. Going small can be a lot of fun. You can even make a tiny series of similar subjects, just like artist Daisy Adams does!

## Go Further

Make a series of paintings of the same object from different views or a portrait from the front and profile views!

# Let's Go!

**Fig. 1:** *Paint in the background on the wood.*

**Fig. 2:** *Cover all of the surface.*

**Fig. 3:** *Start the second layer.*

3. Add the second layer of paint, making sure that you are showing a good range of values (light to dark) and adding details that you feel are important (fig. 3).

4. Cut in the background, by painting in from the edge, if your subject is large and zoomed in, as in this example.

**Fig. 4:** *Use the right brush to make the right mark.*

5. Use an assortment of small brushes, including flats and rounds, to make the strokes you want (fig. 4).

6. When you are finished, paint a protective coating over your artwork with a wide brush, or have an adult spray it with a clear coat as described in Unit 1, page 20.

1. On the gesso-primed piece of wood, begin by working the overall color for the first layer in the background. For our composition, we zoomed into the flower and started with yellow for the petals (fig. 1).

2. Working from the back to the front, add some larger details. Continue until all the surface is covered. Use the tiny brushes to make small strokes, or even dots of color, as you go for details (fig. 2).

## Meet the Artist: Daisy Adams

Daisy Adams is an artist from New Hampshire. She owns a lovely shop called Lucy's Art Emporium, where she sells her work and the work of others in downtown Dover, New Hampshire. Her own work captures the kitschy, vintage feel of wayside America. Her work is often small in size and full of nostalgia.

*Off To See the Wizard* by Daisy Adams

# Painting Like a Fauvist

Materials

- canvas, canvas board, or primed wood
- charcoal
- pencil
- acrylic paints
- variety of bristle brushes
- paper for sketching
- water containers
- newspaper
- paper towels
- photograph of someone
- Plexiglas palette

**Think First:** The Fauvists were known for the wild colors they used on representational images. Often their subject was portraiture. For this lesson, we will work from a photograph. Start by thinking about the emotion the person is projecting in the photo. Is the person mad, sad, silly, or calm? Let the subject's mood guide your color choices. Focus only on the head and shoulders, with a simple background. We chose a girl with a very solemn, almost sad, look on her face.

## Go Further

Make a painting of a favorite place that made you feel a strong emotion. Use your colors to show how it made you feel!

# Let's Go!

Fig. 1: *Sketch the image on the canvas.*

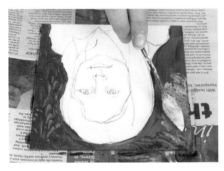

Fig. 2: *Paint in the different shades.*

1. Using a pencil, sketch your idea, without details, onto the painting surface (fig. 1).
2. Set up your painting palette as described in Unit 1, page 20, the acrylic painting section.
3. Think about the colors you want to use to show the person's emotion. Is he or she "red-hot mad" or looking a little "blue"? Perhaps the subject appears to have a "sunny-colored" disposition.

Fig. 3: *Paint the face with your chosen "emotion" colors.*

4. Mix at least four shades of the colors you want to use for your painting (fig. 2).
5. Starting at the background, work around your painting, then fill in with a complementary color to the face. Colors opposite each other on the color wheel are the boldest; colors closer together are less so. See Unit 1, page 22, for more on color (fig. 3).

Fig. 4: *Paint in the final details with a small brush.*

6. Work in the face, neck, and shoulders, using a wide range of light to dark shades. The neck has darker shades cast by the chin; the areas under the sides of the nose are darker—work carefully (fig. 4)!
7. Finish the top layer of paint with details, using smaller brushes and any sort of strokes you like. Seal it when completely dry as described in Unit 1, page 20.

## Meet the Artist: Darryl Joel Berger

About *Yellow Boy,* Darryl Joel Berger says, "It started as a drawing about a specific narrative, a long story I was working on in which Yellow Boy is a character. Sometimes the only way to think of a painting is, does it fully inhabit the space you've given it? I want a painting to be like a window, where everything inside is illuminated and fully alive."

*Yellow Boy* by Darryl Joel Berger

### Materials

- canvas, canvas board, or primed wood
- pencil
- acrylic paints
- variety of bristle brushes
- paper for sketching
- water containers
- newspaper
- paper towels
- photograph of an outdoor location
- Plexiglas palette

**Think First:** This Lab explores what happens when we use complementary colors for the base layer of our painting. This is an age-old technique that can really bring some instant depth to your painting. Find a photograph that really intrigues you and examine the light and color thoroughly. *National Geographic* magazines or photographs of places you have been are great for this.

### Go Further

Try this method with an abstract subject, such as a scribble drawing! (See Lab 3.)

# Let's Go!

***Fig. 1:*** *Sketch the image on the canvas.*

***Fig. 2:*** *Paint in the background.*

***Fig. 3:*** *Use the right shaped brush for the shape area you are painting.*

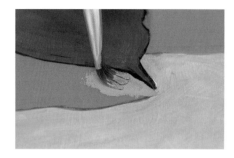

***Fig. 4:*** *Start the second layer with the actual color.*

1. Begin by drawing the horizon line on your canvas. Then include an outline of the most important features (fig. 1).

2. Set up your painting palette as described in Unit 1, page 20, the acrylic painting section.

3. Study the colors in the photograph, and then find a set of complementary colors in your color wheel (see Unit 1, page 22). Use the primary color and its secondary complementary to begin your painting. Start by painting the background (figs. 2 and 3).

4. Work from back to front.

5. Refer to your color wheel to check your opposites! Mix in the complementary color to make the color you are painting with darker—don't use black.

6. When your base is dry, begin again with the sky and paint in the actual colors (fig. 4). Leave some of the underpainting peeking through the edges for contrast.

7. Finish the top layer of paint with small details and let dry. Have an adult seal your painting when completely dry.

## Meet the Artist: Christopher Volpe

"Also a poet, Volpe is drawn to the changing colors, lights, and moods of nature, like dusk and mist. It's the ability of his paintings to exude emotion and movement that distinguishes them from other New England landscapes, as well as a unique perspective and contemporary composition." —Chloe Johnson, journalist

*Beginnings* by Christopher Volpe

# Charcoal and Acrylic Painting

- canvas, canvas board, or primed wood
- charcoal
- pencil
- acrylic paints
- variety of bristle brushes
- water containers
- newspaper
- paper towels
- Plexiglas palette

**Think First:** The subject matter for this Lab is from your imagination. Using a piece of vine charcoal, you will make bold marks to add strength to your artwork. Your imaginary subject can be almost anything: a fantasy animal, landscape, or person!

### Go Further

Try this method with an abstract subject using a limited palette (two complementary colors) for a bold look!

# Let's Go!

**Fig. 1:** *Using the charcoal, make bold marks over the pencil drawing.*

**Fig. 2:** *Fill in the large areas first.*

1. Begin by lightly sketching the main ideas on the canvas with a pencil. Then go over them boldly with the charcoal (fig. 1).

2. Set up your painting palette as described in Unit 1, page 20—dispense most of your colors in small amounts, unless the painting has large areas of one color.

**Fig. 3:** *Mix charcoal with the paint.*

**Fig. 4:** *Put the details back in with the charcoal.*

3. Using your large brushes, fill in the large areas first, working with smaller brushes for the tinier spaces (fig. 2).

4. Work up to the line of charcoal if you do not want to smudge it; paint over the line slightly if you want to soften it. The charcoal will mix with the paint and darken most colors. Add your second layer of paint when everything is dry (fig. 3).

5. Add any details you wish, or go over your charcoal lines to darken them when everything is completely dry (fig. 4).

6. Have an adult seal your painting when completely dry.

## Meet the Author: Susan Schwake

"I like using charcoal to draw back into my paintings. In this painting, *Bluebird*, I used the charcoal to give the shape of the bird a more important role in the overall painting. Birds have been reoccurring themes in my work for thirty years! I enjoy watching them in the wild through binoculars and imagining how it feels to fly."

*Bluebird* by Susan Schwake

# LAB 16 Watercolor and Salt Painting

## Materials

- watercolor paper or cardstock
- set of pan watercolors
- soft-haired watercolor brushes
- small sponge
- newspaper and paper towels
- large water containers
- salt

**Think First:** The subject matter for this painting will come from your imagination. Because the effect of the salt on the watercolor is, in effect, a white or light speck, you might like to think of a subject that involves stars, sparks, tiny lights, snow, or rain. A dark background will render more contrast with the salt. A vibrant color will give a similar effect. Set up your watercolor painting area as described in Unit 1, page 20.

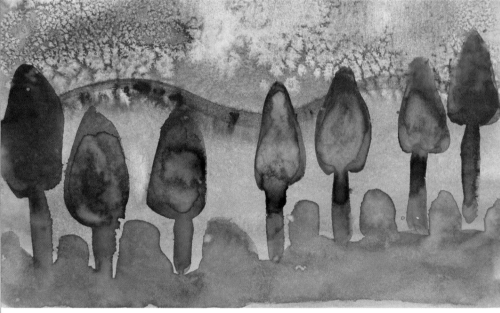

## Go Further

Think of a subject matter for your painting in which the textural effect of salt would be useful: rocks, diamonds, caves, castles, sand, and fantasy creatures!

# Let's Go!

*Fig. 1: Begin painting with a very wet brush.*

*Fig. 2: Sprinkle the salt.*

*Fig. 3: See how the salt has moved the pigment.*

1. Use your brush or a clean sponge to wet the paper. The brush should be wet, but not soggy!

2. Wet your brush again, and start to paint in your colors (fig. 1).

3. While the paint is still wet, but not in puddles, put some salt in one hand, and, using a pinching motion with your fingers, sprinkle it lightly in the areas where you want the effect. Deep, rich colors will produce a more vivid effect with the salt (fig. 2).

4. Remember, less is more—in the amount of salt and the amount of water.

5. When your painting is completely dry, rub the salt from the surface of the paper.

6. Admire the textural effect that salt has on your painting (fig. 3).

## Meet the Author: Susan Schwake

"I have often used salt for texture in my watercolor work. This can be seen in the background of this collage illustration, *Evening Song*. I wanted to add interest to the watery lake and sky melting together, so I used salt to texture the two elements into one. I also had the lucky bonus of a rock shape appearing in the salt for the cricket to sit on."

*Evening Song* by Susan Schwake

# Watercolor and Plastic Painting

**Think First:** Choose your favorite color combinations in your paint set. Think of how they might look together and how you would like to place them on your paper. Decide if you are going to mix new colors from the set for these artworks. Gather your supplies and set up a watercolor painting area as described in Unit 1, page 20. Cut plenty of plastic wrap to the size of the paper ahead of time—one piece sized for each piece of paper to be painted.

- heavy paper for watercolor
- plastic wrap
- watercolors
- soft brushes
- containers of water
- newspaper and paper towels
- scissors
- glue stick for gluing paper

## Go Further

Use black ink to make a drawing over a painting you are not satisfied with. It's good to turn a piece of art you don't love into something else!

# Let's Go!

Fig. 1: Start with a wet brush on wet paper.

Fig. 2: This wet-on-wet technique allows for spontaneous mixing!

1. Use your brush to wet the paper. If your paper is large, wet it with a clean sponge.

2. Using a very wet brush and your predetermined color schemes, stroke the watercolor pans with your brush to load it with color.

3. Paint the color into the areas, filling the paper completely with as many or as few colors as you like (fig. 1).

4. Because the paper is wet and so is the paint, spreading will occur. This is called wet on wet and is a good thing! (fig. 2).

Fig. 3: Apply plastic wrap.

5. While the paper is still wet, place the plastic wrap over the painting with your hands and let it fully contact the paper. (fig. 3). Wrinkles are good. Encourage them by tickling the plastic wrap a bit (fig. 4).

Fig. 4: Encourage wrinkles by squeezing together areas of the plastic wrap.

6. Do this to all of your papers. Let them all dry overnight. Don't peek!

7. Peel off the plastic in the morning and find your beautiful paintings waiting for you!

8. Keep the plastic wrap in a folder for the next time you want to make these paintings.

## Meet the Author: Susan Schwake

"I often like to work with this watercolor method to create specific elements for my collages. I often tend to find insects, wings, ice, windows, and rocks in my paintings with this process. You can see this in my illustration entitled *Night Flight*."

*Night Flight* by Susan Schwake

# 18 Tempera Trees, Gouache Skies

**Materials**

- watercolor paper
- pencil
- tempera or gouache paints
- variety of soft brushes
- water containers
- newspaper
- paper towels
- gel pens or fine ballpoint pens
- Plexiglas welled palette

**Think First:** For this painting, we will paint in a more primitive style. For subject matter, you will identify something iconic or native to where you live. Using a photograph, book, or sketch you have made, simplify the idea into a more-basic form, but keep the key details that make it special. The tempera and gouache paints are matte and flat-looking, which lends a more illustrative look to the painting. For our example, we used a book of animals for a reference for our local crustacean, the lobster!

## Go Further

Make a series of small paintings on paper or primed wood depicting a collection of small, still-life objects, like artist Lisa Congdon does.

# Let's Go!

Fig. 1: Sketch out your idea.

Fig. 2: Mix gouache in a small, welled palette.

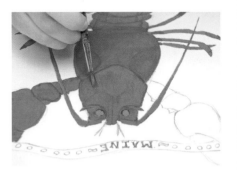

Fig. 4: Directly mix the colors on the paper.

1. Using a pencil, lay out your painting on the paper (fig. 1).

2. Set up your painting palette as described in Unit 1, page 20, using a small-welled palette (fig. 2).

3. Work in areas separate from one another—this paint is a lot like watercolor and will run if wet paint touches a wet area (fig. 3).

4. Fill in all of your areas with color, working wet next to dry.

5. You can mix the colors as you go directly in the wet work or in the wells before applying (fig. 4).

6. When the painting is dry, add outlines or details with the gel pens or ballpoint pens (fig. 5).

Fig. 3: Paint in separate areas so the paint does not blend.

Fig. 5: Add details with the pens.

## Meet the Artist: Lisa Congdon

San Francisco illustrator and fine artist Lisa Congdon was raised in upstate New York and in Northern California, where she grew to love the trees and animals that surrounded her. That love is expressed most intensely through her gouache paintings and pencil drawings.

Nautical Managerie by Lisa Condgon

# Marker and Acrylic Painting

- canvas, canvas board, or primed wood
- pencil
- black permanent marker
- acrylic paint
- bristle brushes
- newspaper and paper towels
- water and containers
- Plexiglas palette
- mirror

**Think First:** This lesson encourages you to draw and to paint on the canvas, creating a modern, heavily outlined portrait. Using the mirror, examine your face and the shapes you can find in it. Your face will have one shape—your eyes, mouth, and nose other shapes. We will keep the contemporary graphic style of eliminating the background to focus on the portrait itself. Choose a background color before beginning.

## Go Further

Try painting a group of your friends in this fashion. Work from a photo or ask them to pose for your pencil sketch!

# Let's Go!

*Fig. 1:* Use the black permanent marker over the pencil lines.

*Fig. 2:* Paint in the background.

*Fig. 3:* Paint a range of values of skin tone.

*Fig. 4:* Paint in the clothing.

1. In pencil, make a light drawing of yourself on the canvas.

2. Go over the lines with the black permanent marker (fig. 1).

3. Set up your palette as described in Unit 1, page 20, for acrylic paint. Paint the background first with your solid color (fig. 2).

4. Mix your flesh tones to create a few shades of the color you wish to use for your skin tones. Paint these in next. Feel free to use the range of values found on your face (fig. 3).

5. Finish with your features and clothing (fig. 4). Go over any black lines that you painted over. Seal as described in Unit 1, page 20.

## Meet the Artist: Darryl Joel Berger

Darryl Joel Berger is an artist and writer who works and lives in Ontario, Canada. Of his painting, Darryl says, "In many ways, this is really a drawing. I wanted to make something bold and graphic, something simplified and direct, like the best drawings can be. At the same time, I wanted to keep the kind of weight and thoughtfulness that you (should) find in paintings, so I applied the color in an abstract way, with plenty of power and movement." Find out more about Darryl at: http://red-handed.blogspot.com.

*Pow Wow* by Darryl Joel Berger

# 20 Watercolor Shapes

- watercolor paper, 90-lb. or more
- watercolor pans
- soft-haired watercolor brushes
- newspaper
- paper towels
- large containers of water

**Think First:** This lesson is experimental and process-oriented, allowing you to create an abstract, pattern-based painting. Start by selecting three to five favorite colors for your palette. Think of shapes you would like to include in this painting.

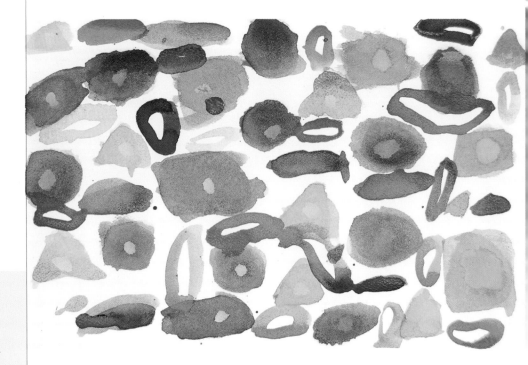

## Go Further

- Paint large shapes that are filled in with one color. Let them dry completely, and then paint open-contour shapes over them.
- Make a painting with a limited palette of two colors.

# Let's Go!

Fig. 1: Start anywhere on your paper with
your first color.

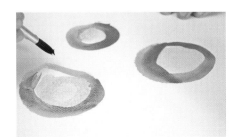

Fig. 2: Repeat shapes in different sizes
and colors.

Fig. 3: Try painting different shapes.

Fig. 4: Paint next to a dry area,

Fig. 5: Finish your painting.

1. Load up a wet brush with your first color.
2. Starting anywhere on your paper, create
   areas of shapes and color (fig. 1).
3. Use a repeated shape in different sizes
   and colors to fill in areas. Use both light
   and dark values for the most impact
   (fig. 2).
4. Try painting different shapes together in
   the same colors, or paint the same
   shape in different sizes (fig. 3).
5. Let the watercolor paint dry before
   painting right next to it since wet areas
   that touch will run together (fig. 4).
6. Continue until the painting is as full as
   you wish (fig. 5)!

## Meet the Artist:
## Heather Smith Jones

Heather Smith Jones is an artist, arts instructor,
and author from Lawrence, Kansas. Her work,
entitled *Keep Going When You Are Not Sure,* is
an inspiration for creating this lesson. It's
important to always keep moving forward with
your artwork. See more of Heather's beautiful
work at heathersmithjones.com.

*Keep Going When You Are Not Sure*
by Heather Smith Jones

# fingertip Painting on Wood

## Materials

- a piece of cast-off, smooth wood
- gesso
- larger bristle or foam brush about 2" (5.1 cm)
- acrylic paints
- small damp sponge
- newspaper
- Plexiglas palette
- paper towels
- sketching paper
- pencil
- flower catalogs, live flowers, or photographs of flowers

### Go further

- Make a triptych of vertical rectangles to create a larger artwork.
- Make a large number of artworks to group together on a wall, as in a garden.

**Think First:** An hour or more ahead of time, prime your wood with gesso using the large bristle or foam brush. Paint a wide stripe of gesso down the middle, leaving 1" (5 cm) on each side of the wood showing. When the gesso is dry, cover your work area with newspapers. Set up your palette area, with a piece of Plexiglas for your paints. Dispense some red, yellow, blue, and white acrylic paints—use about a 1" (2.5 cm) circle to start— and have a small damp sponge handy to clean your fingertip between colors.

Study the reference materials and choose your favorite flowers to paint. Take a look at the size of your found wood. Is it tall enough for the type of flowers you chose? Using pencil and paper, sketch a few ideas of what your painting could look like. Chose your favorite sketch and get out your prepared board.

# Let's Go!

*Fig. 1:* Dip just the end of the finger into the paint.

In this painting, the flowers are the main attraction. We will begin by painting them the same way they grow. This alternative method of painting and mixing colors is a great way to get started painting without the stress of learning how to choose and use brushes.

1. Starting with the stems and leaves, pick up blue paint on the tip of your finger and paint a dot at the bottom of the stem. Work your way up a little at a time, using this dot method (fig. 1).

2. While the blue paint is still wet, clean your fingertip on the damp sponge and then dry it on a paper towel. Pick up some yellow paint and mix it into the blue paint on the flower stem. Using an up-and-down "tapping motion," mix the paint to make the stem green. More yellow paint will make the stem lighter; less yellow will make it darker. Try shading the leaves or the stem using this method of light and dark. Continue painting the stems and

*Fig. 2:* Use an up-and-down tapping motion for applying and mixing the colors.

*Fig. 3:* Shape the blooms.

leaves until you are finished with them. Wiping your finger between colors keeps your palette neat and prepares you for the new color of the blooms (fig. 2).

3. Carefully examine the colors and shapes of your blooms. Again, use a small amount of paint on your fingertip and shape the blooms with the tapping/dotting motion. Try using different fingers to vary sizes of petals and leaves.

Use white to make tints of the colors you mix, but always use yellow to lighten your greens. Blue and red will make purples. Red and yellow will make oranges. When mixing shades of color, avoid mixing the colors thoroughly for a mottled look (fig. 3).

## Meet the Artist: Amy Rice

Amy Rice is an artist from Minneapolis, Minnesota. Her mixed-media painting, *Zinnias*, was made on an old piece of found barn board wood. This work inspired the fingertip painting project! See more of her work at www.amyrice.com.

# Printmaking

**MAKING ART MULTIPLES IS AN ADDICTIVE PROCESS** for most people. Printmaking is instant gratification at the most basic level, with the element of chance enhancing the technical process. The ability to create multiples of your artful idea—from a simple fingerprint to a sophisticated multi-plate foam print—is intriguing. This Unit explores many printmaking processes without the use of a press, from singular monotypes to multiple serigraph prints, to help students learn how to think in reverse, or in layers. A variety of papers and methods will produce endless variations on a theme from each Lab.

UNIT 4

# Found Objects Prints

- printmaking, sketch, or other smooth, medium-weight paper
- water-based printmaking ink in any color
- Plexiglas palette
- soft brayer(s)
- shallow dish of water
- paper towels
- newspaper
- white test paper
- objects to print, as described in Unit 1, page 17

**Think First:** Study your objects and arrange them on your test paper. Do they make a face or a pattern? On the Plexiglas, roll out a small amount (a 1" [2.5 cm] circle) of any color of ink. Make sure it is somewhat smooth. Using the brayer, apply some ink to the object. Print the object onto the test paper to see the mark it makes. Experiment with the different objects you have chosen, and see what you can build with the marks you print. Try printing with only one "inking," to make lighter and lighter impressions, or use more or less pressure on the object when printing. Think about what a repeated pattern can do, too!

## Meet the Artist: Terry Winters

Terry Winters is an American artist who works in printmaking, painting, and drawing. His *Folio* series inspired the circular prints in the Go Further section of this Lab. For more information on Terry Winters, visit www.moma.org.

# Let's Go!

*Test the print that each object makes first to plan your artwork.*

**Fig. 1:** *Roll out the ink slowly and smoothly.*

Prepare your area for printmaking as described on page 23. When you have decided on the subject or pattern you want to print, you are ready to begin.

1. On the Plexiglas, roll out the other colors you will use (fig. 1).

2. Using the brayer, apply ink in a smooth rolling motion to one side of the object. Dipping objects in the ink can result in too much ink, so try the brayer first. For

**Fig. 2:** *Use the brayer to apply the ink to the object.*

**Fig. 3:** *Use firm, steady pressure to print your object.*

a crisp, clear print of the object, less ink is better than too much ink (fig. 2).

3. Press the object onto the paper with a firm motion. Continue making your prints, using the brayer to apply the ink, until your piece is finished (fig. 3).

4. Let the print dry for several hours or overnight, either on a flat surface or hanging from a line with a clip.

## Go Further

- Try lace or other textured fabric on your print.

- Use the same object over and over to create a large area of one pattern.

- Your prints can go around and around a shaped piece of paper.

# Serigraphs/Silk Screen

- white or light-colored fabric
- wax paper
- sketch paper
- printing paper
- pencil
- nonwater-soluble glue (I like Mod Podge)
- acrylic paint
- acrylic textile medium
- newspaper
- paper towels
- Plexiglas palette
- sheer curtain or silk-screening material
- wooden embroidery hoop
- small bristle brush

**Think First:** Silk screening or serigraph is a stencil method of printmaking. You create a positive image by blocking out the negative space on the screen and pushing the ink through the remaining holes to create an easily repeatable print. You can use a simple design, with medium thick lines, and even text, if you desire. You can print on both paper and fabric, as we did. You can even make your own hand-printed shirts and scarves with this method.

## Go Further

You can silk screen onto almost anything. Try making your own stationery, or put your own design on the edge of a tablecloth. Make a set of napkins to match.

# Let's Go!

**Fig. 1:** *Sketch out your idea first.*

**Fig. 2:** *Trace your idea onto the fabric carefully.*

1. Draw your design inside a circle you have traced inside your embroidery hoop. Leave at least a 1" (2.5 cm) border all the way around the edge of your design (fig. 1).

2. Put your curtain or screening fabric in the hoop and tighten it well. Place it directly on the drawing and trace the design (fig. 2).

3. Using a piece of waxed paper underneath the hoop, apply the glue with a small brush. Block out the areas that you do not want to print. Check that all the holes are filled by holding it up to the light. Let the glue dry completely (fig. 3).

**Fig. 3:** *Apply the glue with a small brush.*

4. Mix two parts textile medium to one part acrylic paint. The mixture should be as thick as heavy cream. Lay your hoop on the surface to be printed. Using a bristle brush, paint the mixture with even strokes through your embroidery hoop stencil. Using a back-and-forth stroke gives you the most even print (fig. 4).

**Fig. 4:** *Use a bristle brush to paint through the screen.*

5. Lift the hoop when you are sure you have gone over all the areas thoroughly. Clean the screen well with the spray attachment on your sink, until the holes are all clear.

6. Let dry. Use a dry iron to set the print if you have printed on fabric.

## Meet the Artist: Megan Bogonovich

Megan Bogonovich is a New Hampshire artist who introduced me to silk screening on clay. (But that is another lesson for another book.) Her work with silk screening on clay and her big ceramic sculptures have drawn international attention. She is a fearless artist, who I greatly admire. In the work shown here, she has silk screened her family photos directly onto the porcelain. See more of her fantastic work at www.meganbogonovich.com.

*Family Jar with Lid* by Megan Bogonovich

- heavyweight drawing paper
- liquid acrylic paint
- paint cups
- cotton string
- scissors
- craft sticks

**Think First:** This is a spontaneous and physical art process. Participants should be standing up if possible and, if the space allows, using full arm motions! Choose your colors ahead of time and cut the string into lengths as long as your forearm.

### Meet the Artist:
### Jackson Pollock

Jackson Pollock is known for his layers of spatter-like paintings. Rich layers of color were applied through dripping sticks and holes in paint buckets swung over canvases laid out on the artist's studio floor. His work inspired this Lab. For more information on Jackson Pollock's work, visit the Museum of Modern Art in New York City, or online at moma.org.

# Let's Go!

*Fig. 1:* Dip your string into the paint.

*Fig. 2:* Immerse the string with a craft stick.

1. Dip your string into the paint (fig. 1).
2. Using a craft stick, immerse and coat the string with the paint (fig. 2).
3. Holding the string above your paper, let your arm drop and let the string go limp onto the paper (fig. 3).
4. Continue with this motion until you are ready to change colors (fig. 4).
5. Use one string per color to avoid mixing.

*Fig. 3:* Drop the string onto the paper.

*Fig. 4:* Continue to add colors.

*Fig. 5:* Move the string in different directions.

6. Another method of printing is to drag the string across the paper (fig. 5).

## Go Further

- Fold the paper over the string and hold the paper with your hand while you pull out the string.
- Fill the paper fully with one method, let it dry, then use another method on top.

# Polystyrene Plate Printing

## Materials

- thin copy paper
- pencil or ballpoint pen
- polystyrene tray
- water-based printmaking ink any color
- printing paper
- masking tape
- newspaper
- paper towels
- brayer

**Think First:** Printing with polystyrene plates is a relief print process, much like a lino or woodcut print. You carve into the foam to make a line, and, when printed, the carved parts remain the color of the paper. It is easy for anyone to do, because polystyrene is a soft material and is easily carved using any sort of hard point. For this lesson, we will use a pencil or ballpoint pen.

From your imagination, sketch out an idea for a small series of prints. For this example, we made two different designs for our printing plate subjects: a rabbit and a little alien being.

## Go Further

Younger children or first-time artists might like to use texture tools (see Printmaking in Unit 1, page 23 ) to make their first plates. These will print as fun, abstract works.

# Let's Go!

**Fig. 1:** *Sketch out the idea.*

**Fig. 3:** *Carve into the plate.*

**Fig. 4:** *Rub the plate with your fingertips.*

**Fig. 2:** *Cut off the rounded edges of the plate.*

1. With a pencil, get your idea down on the copy paper. Prepare your printing paper as described in Unit 1, page 23 (fig. 1).

2. Snap or cut off the curved sides of a polystyrene tray to make a flat printing plate (fig. 2).

3. Tape your drawing over the polystyrene plate and, using a ballpoint pen or firm hand on the pencil, retrace your lines to carve into the plate (fig. 3).

4. Lift the paper and check your carving lines. Make sure they are deep enough to be felt easily when you run your finger over them. If not, go over them again without the paper on top.

5. Prepare your ink for printing as described in Unit 1, page 23. Roll the ink onto the printing plate smoothly and evenly.

6. Place the printing paper over the plate or flip the plate over onto the paper (fig. 4).

7. Rub the plate or the paper with your fingertips in a circular motion all over and to the edges (fig. 4). Peel off the paper to reveal your print.

8. Re-ink the plate and repeat with new paper sheets to complete your printing edition. Let dry several hours or overnight.

## Meet the Artist: Annette Mitchell

Professor Annette Mitchell published a book and a DVD about her printmaking process, which uses polystyrene as a block-printing medium.

*In Our Own Private Worlds* by Annette Mitchell

# Monotypes

## Materials

- polystyrene tray for ink
- Plexiglas
- pencil with an eraser on the end
- water-based printmaking ink
- lightweight printing paper
- newspaper
- wet paper towel
- masking tape
- brayer

**Think First:** Making monotypes can be a spontaneous art form, with the center of the process deeply rooted in play. Mono, meaning "one," tells you that these are one-of-a-kind prints. There are many ways to make monotypes—this is only one, but it's a simple, fun way to explore the process. It's drawing and thinking in reverse, with the elements of chance thrown in. Try to keep the expectations loose, and focus on the fun. Pick a general idea of subject matter to draw from, and plan to make quite a few prints.

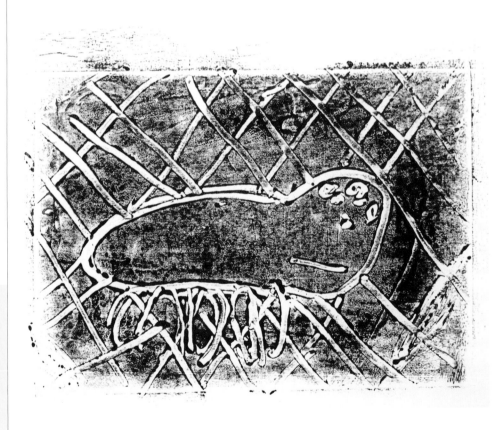

### Go Further

Younger children or first-time artists might like to use texture tools (see Printmaking in Unit 1, page 23 ) to make their first plates.

# Let's Go!

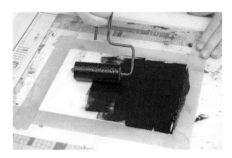

*Fig. 1:* Roll the ink onto the plate.

*Fig. 2:* Draw into the plate with a pencil point.

*Fig. 3:* Draw into the plate with an eraser.

1. Begin by taping off an area on the Plexiglas that is a little smaller than your paper size. This will leave a nice border around your image.
2. Roll out your prepared ink on the polystyrene tray as described in Unit 1, page 23. Next, roll the ink within the taped area on your Plexiglas plate (fig. 1).

3. Using your pencil and the eraser, draw into the ink. The eraser will make a thick, soft line, the pencil point a thinner one (figs. 2, 3).
4. Center your printing paper over the image and carefully place it onto the plate. Rub the paper all over with your hands, being careful not to move the paper on the plate (fig. 4).
5. Peel off the paper, then sign and number your new monotype!

*Fig. 4:* Rub the back of the paper with your hands.

## Meet the Artist:
## Edibeth Farrington

Edibeth Farrington is an artist and art educator who lives and works in New Hampshire. "I have always loved print-making," she says, "but I especially love the spontaneity of monotypes. Immediate and satisfying, a monotype can tie together loose ends of previous work or propel me into the new."

*Phone Home* by Edibeth Farrington

# Fruit and Vegetable Prints

- assorted colors or white printing papers
- block printing ink
- forks for use as handles in the big fruits
- Plexiglas palette
- brayer
- newspaper
- an assortment of produce, such as lemons, mushrooms, peppers, apples, lettuce, and celery

**Think First:** Cut each fruit or vegetable so it has an even edge for printing. Lettuce is the exception to this rule. Onions make a great print, but they can make some people cry. Try them if you dare! Each piece of produce makes its own distinctive print. Consider combining shapes to make something representational, or make beautiful repeated patterns with the shapes. Using a fork as a handle in the larger fruits makes them easier to hold and print.

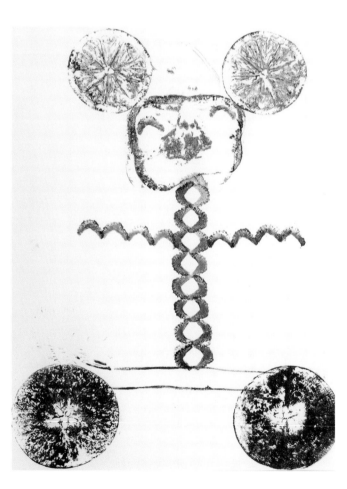

## Go Further

These prints can make wonderful greeting cards or gift wrap.

# Let's Go!

***Fig. 1:*** *Roll the ink onto the produce.*

***Fig. 2:*** *Press firmly!*

***Fig. 3:*** *Repeat the printing process.*

1. Prepare your area for printmaking as described on page 23. Roll some ink onto Plexiglas.
2. Using the brayer, apply ink to the produce (fig. 1).

3. Make your print by pressing the produce firmly onto the paper (fig. 2).
4. Re-ink and keep going (fig. 3)!

5. Let the prints dry for several hours or overnight.

## Meet the Artists: My Students

My students have made so many beautiful prints. I am featuring one of my favorites: a celery and mushroom forest. Colorful ink can be a fun change from black and white!

Colorful fruit and vegetable prints created by my students

## Materials

- cardstock
- optional: wax paper
- pan watercolors
- black block-printing ink
- Plexiglas palette
- brayer
- newspaper
- paper towels
- assortment of leaves

**Think First:** Collect a selection of leaves in a variety of shapes. You can even try long-needled pine leaves and flat seed pods. Decide on some color themes for your background paper. You can use one color family, such as oranges, reds, and yellows, or paint a rainbow of colors!

### Go Further

You can print leaves onto a T-shirt by using the textile medium and acrylic paint as described in Lab 23. For washability, set the ink with an iron set on medium-high. Use a piece of paper inside the shirt and pass the iron over the print for three minutes.

# Let's Go!

*Fig. 1:* Paint the cardstock.

*Fig. 2:* Roll the ink onto the leaf.

1. Paint your cardstock with your choice of colors and patterns (fig. 1).
2. Let the paper dry completely and prepare your ink as described in Unit 1, page 23.
3. With the back side of the leaf up, roll the ink-loaded brayer over the leaf, coating it fully (fig. 2).

4. Print the leaf by placing it on the paper (fig. 3). Rub it gently but firmly, to make a great print. You can use wax paper over the leaf to keep your hands free from ink.
5. Continue printing until you are satisfied with the final piece.
6. Let it dry for several hours or overnight.

*Fig. 3:* Print the leaf.

## Meet the Artist: Judith Heller Cassell

Judith Heller Cassell is a celebrated artist and member of the Boston Printmakers Association. This beautiful 3' x 4' (0.9 x 1.2 m) print hung in our gallery studio and inspired this lesson. Judith's prints are often in our studio gallery.

*Persimmon Gold* a monotype woodcut by Judith Heller Cassell

# Cardboard Relief Print

Materials

**Materials**

- matboard or a strong piece of cardboard
- printing paper
- black block-printing ink
- Plexiglas palette
- brayer
- clear or white glue
- gesso and gesso brush
- an assortment of cardboard pieces

**Think First:** Sort through the cardboard pieces, and peel back some of the top layers to expose the corrugated part. Decide on a subject matter for your print—abstract is fun to begin with! You can sketch out a few ideas first of shapes you might use, if that helps your creative process.

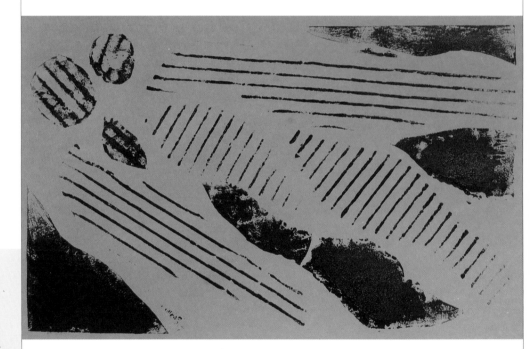

## Go Further

These prints can be made with representational subjects, such as a landscape, a still life, or even a portrait. Just use the essence of the shapes for the best results.

# Let's Go!

*Fig. 1:* Expose the corrugated surface.

*Fig. 2:* Lay out and glue the pieces.

1. Cut out your cardboard shapes. Peel away the top layer of some pieces to expose the corrugated surface; leave some pieces smooth (fig. 1).

2. Lay the pieces out on the matboard and glue them down. This will be your printing plate (fig. 2).

3. Let the glue dry completely, then gesso over the whole plate (fig. 3).

*Fig. 3:* Paint the gesso on the printing plate.

*Fig. 4:* Roll out the ink on the plate.

4. Prepare and apply the ink to the printing plate as described in Unit 1, page 23 (fig. 4).

5. Position the printing paper onto the plate and hold it with one hand, while rubbing over the paper in circular motions with the other hand. Peel off the paper to reveal your new print!

6. Continue with your prints to make an edition, as described in Unit 1, page 23.

7. Let them dry for several hours or overnight.

## Meet the Artist: John Terry Downs

John Terry Downs was and is to this day my favorite art teacher. He was my professor for figure drawing and print-making and might be the best art teacher in the world. His prints, drawings, and paintings have been shown all over the world and have inspired hundreds of students. More about John can be found at www.plymouth.edu/department/art/faculty/profile/john-t-downs.

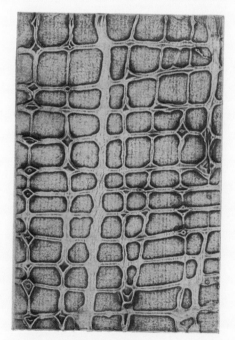

A collagraph print called *Pink Grid* by John Terry Downs

# Stencil Me This

- freezer paper
- a piece of white cotton
- acrylic paint
- textile medium
- Plexiglas palette
- small bristle brush
- scissors
- iron
- newspaper
- embroidery hoop for display

**Think First:** Stencils are ancient in origin and have been used in a variety of fine art movements throughout the twentieth century—think Warhol and, before that, the posters of the art deco movement. Stencil images can be made over and over with a plastic stencil or, as in this lesson, just once, but very easily, with a paper stencil. All parts of the stencil need to be joined, or you will need a bridge connecting the parts (think of the lowercase letter e with a space being a bridge between the cross part of the e so it doesn't touch the curved part) or a floating separate piece called an island (think of the letter O as a donut and the island being the "hole"). For this lesson we are using a landscape motif created without islands or bridges.

## Go Further

Think about adding words and letters to your stencil if you have something to say—just like Sub-studio did.

# Let's Go!

*Fig. 1: Draw the image on the freezer paper.*

*Fig. 2: Cut out the stencil.*

1. Draw your image on the non-shiny side of the freezer paper (fig. 1).

2. Cut into the paper in a line from the bottom edge to access the image (fig. 2).

3. When the design is cut out, place the large piece with the hole on your fabric, shiny side down. With a medium-hot iron, press the stencil firmly, right to the edge of the freezer paper. It should adhere fully.

4. Using the iron, seal off the bottom of the image with an additional strip of

*Fig. 3: Apply the paint to the stencil.*

*Fig. 4: Peel off the freezer paper after the paint is dry.*

freezer paper to cover your initial cut into the paper.

5. Mix two parts textile medium to one part acrylic paint until blended.

6. Apply the paint with a bristle brush, starting at the edges of the stencil and working inward (fig. 3).

7. Finish painting all the areas and let dry for several hours or overnight. Peel off the freezer paper to reveal your print (fig. 4).

8. Stretch the fabric in the embroidery hoop and cut off the excess, if necessary.

## Meet the Artist: Sub-studio

Sub-studio was formed in 2006, when Anna Corpron and Sean Auyeung forged a design partnership to combine their individual creative interests. "At the moment, we draw inspiration from the flora and fauna of the natural world, urban spaces, and the creatures we imagine. We love screenprinting as a medium because of the element of surprise that it brings to the process."

*Wise Old Owl* by Sub-studio

# LAB 31 Gelatin Printing

## Materials

- printmaking paper or copy paper to start
- block-printing ink
- brayer
- gelatin plate (see Unit 1, page 23)
- paper towels
- Plexiglas palette
- small soft-bristle brush
- scissors
- scrap paper for stencils
- newspaper
- assortment of found objects (see Unit 1, page 17)

**Think First:** Gelatin printing is my favorite method for making prints. The ink floats on the surface of the gelatin and can be manipulated gently for a long time, because it keeps the ink moist. It is exciting and contagious, so prepare to have a lot of paper—and time—on hand! It takes a few prints to get the hang of it, but once you do, it's all fun and games. This method of printmaking has many additional steps to explore, but for this Lab, we will do the simplest forms.

To create your design, use a brush or the eraser on the end of a pencil—it has the most natural feel in your hand. Also, printing from a gelatin plate makes everything backwards—create your design with that in mind. Most important, remember that the plate is just gelatin, so you must be gentle with it.

## Go Further

Cut up some paper stencils and place them on the gelatin to block the ink. Try inking them first with another color, too, for a different look.

# Let's Go!

*Fig. 1: Roll the ink onto the plate.*

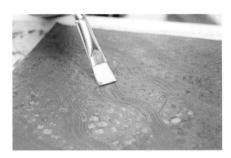

*Fig. 2: Apply ink with a brush.*

1. Make the gelatin plate as described in Unit 1, page 23.

2. Roll out some ink on your palette. Less is more here! Then roll the ink in a very thin layer onto the gelatin plate (fig. 1).

3. You can use multiple colors of ink on your plate, overlapping or not! Using a brush, gently (remember, it's just gelatin!) paint away the color to make an image—or add another color to the plate with the brush (fig. 2).

*Fig. 3: Use a cork to print circles.*

4. If you prefer, you can use found objects (none that will scratch the gelatin) and print onto the plate (fig. 3).

5. When you are satisfied with the surface, place your paper over the gelatin plate and gently smooth the back of the paper with your hands (fig. 4).

## Meet the Author: Susan Schwake

"I have been making gelatin prints off and on for twenty years. The print here, *Birds in the Bush*, was made for The Working Proof's Japan earthquake relief fundraiser. It was reproduced as a digital print to raise money for Doctor's Without Borders. (Visit www.theworkingproof .com for more beautiful prints.) I kept the original gelatin print and have it hanging in my home to remind me that, no matter how long the winter, spring will always come again."

*Fig. 4: Print the plate.*

6. Peel off the paper to reveal your print! Begin again with the remaining ink, adding to the plate, or wipe gently with a damp paper towel. Make a lot of prints—it takes a while to get used to the process. Store your gelatin plate in the refrigerator for up to one week.

*Birds in the Bush* by Susan Schwake

# Paper

**PAPER IS A STAPLE IN THE ART STUDIO,** and most art budgets can include paper as a material for creating artwork. This Unit explores using paper as the medium for a substrate, as a structure, and for color, texture, and value. We will create collages, masks, and monsters from recycled maps, magazines, and other printed materials, as well as for your own textured papers. Paper can be used in art forms in endless ways. These Labs are springboards to other places, in which you can experiment with paper further and transform it with other media.

UNIT

5

# Foamy Stamps

- cardstock
- craft foam with sticky backing
- foamcore or cardboard
- pencil
- ballpoint pen
- ink pads
- watercolor pans
- soft-bristle brush
- scissors
- newspaper

**Think First:** Making your own rubber stamps is a fun way to make multiple images. The craft foam is easy for hands of all sizes to cut and yields to a ballpoint pen for carving in details. The sticky backside also adheres easily to cardboard or foamcore, which gives the stamp a handle. Decide what you would like to make a print of, over and over. We chose the sea as our theme: fish, lobster, sharks, and seaweed! You can print on papers that you have made (as in Lab 41), or simply use the watercolors to make a background of your choice as you go.

## Go Further

We made some little fish cards and bookmarks by simply folding the cardstock or cutting it to size. You can stamp your design onto an endless number of things!

# Let's Go!

**Fig. 1:** *Draw your ideas on the paper side of the foam.*

**Fig. 2:** *Cut the stamp out.*

1. Draw your image on the backside of the foam, where the paper covers the sticky side (fig. 1).
2. Cut the images from the foam (fig. 2).
3. Using your ballpoint pen, add the details you want on the foamy side. Press hard (fig. 3).

**Fig. 3:** *Use a ballpoint pen to carve in details.*

4. When you are done with your stamp, peel off the paper and press it firmly onto the foamcore or cardboard.
5. Choose an ink color to print your stamp with. Press it into the ink pad, then print it onto your paper (fig. 4).

**Fig. 4:** *Print your stamp.*

6. When you want to change color or finish your printing run, clean off the stamp with an alcohol wipe.
7. For a different look, try painting the paper first with watercolors. Let dry and print with stamps.

## Meet the Artist:
## Noelle Griskey of Pink Bathtub

About her work, Noelle Griskey says, "My work comes from an appreciation for the little things in life. I am constantly inspired by everyday objects, and my intention is to make the ordinary interesting." See more of Noelle's work at her website: www.pinkbathtub.com

*Mason Jar with Fireflies* by Noelle Griskey

# Large-Scale Paper Fish

## Materials

- 2 large sheets of white, heavyweight paper
- pencil
- watercolor pans
- soft-bristle brush
- scissors
- oil pastels
- newspaper
- paper towels
- heavy string

**Think First:** Your fish can be modeled on a real fish or made up from your imagination, just like we did in this Lab. Even the youngest artist can make a very big fish, with a little help from an older child. Examine some real fish in a tank or in a science book to figure out what shape to make your fish's scales. What color is your fish? What size fins and eyes will it have? Decide on the type of fish you want to make, and let's get started.

## Go Further

You can make smaller versions of this fish and create a mobile, by hanging multiples from a branch you have found outside! Use tissue paper to stuff them.

# Let's Go!

*Fig. 1: Draw in the details with oil pastels.*

*Fig. 3: Paint the fish.*

*Fig. 4: Staple around the edges of the fish.*

*Fig. 2: Cut out the fish.*

the whole fish with watercolor. The oil pastel will resist the watercolor and you will see your drawings perfectly (fig. 3).

**6.** When the fish is dry, staple it together, stapling most of the way around the edge of the fish, but leaving a gap. Get some help from an older friend, if you need it (fig. 4).

**7.** Wad up some newspaper into small balls and feed the fish until he is as fat as you wish him to be (fig. 5). Staple him shut, and hang him from a string!

*Fig. 5: Stuff the fish with newspaper.*

**1.** Tape the two pieces of paper together. Draw the outline of the fish on the top piece with a pencil.

**2.** Add color with the oil pastels (fig. 1).

**3.** Using the scissors, cut the fish from the papers, being sure to cut through both pieces (fig. 2).

**4.** When the fish is free from the paper, open it flat to draw the other side.

**5.** Draw the other side of the fish with the oil pastels, as you did on the first side. Then, with the paper open flat, paint

## Meet the Artist: Ulla Milbrath

Ulla Norup Milbrath taught high school art and ceramics and now teaches a variety of arts, including paper and fiber arts, jewelry design, and paper-clay sculpting in her studio in Northern California and at Castle in the Air studio in Berkeley, California.

*Fabric Koi by Ulla Milbrath*

# LAB 34 Collage Tissue Self-Portraits

## Materials

- paper
- pencil
- newspaper
- white glue
- water
- small container
- soft-bristle brush
- scissors
- tissue paper in assorted colors
- mirror

### Meet the Artist: Chuck Close

Chuck Close uses many different kinds of materials to make his portraits. In a portrait of his daughter, Georgia, he used more than thirty shades of gray paper to construct his 54" x 36" (137 x 99.5 cm) collage. His work is exhibited in many museums worldwide. To see it, visit a museum or check out the Internet.

**Think First:** Did you know that you can mix colors with transparent tissue paper, just like paint? It's true! This lesson uses tissue paper, for the color and texture of the artwork, and glue, to hold the color in place. You can go with your natural colors or make yourself into a fantasy character, as our example shows.

# Let's Go!

**Fig. 1:** *Draw yourself with a mirror.*

**Fig. 2:** *Glue the tissue.*

**Fig. 3:** *Glue and layer the tissue.*

1. Start by taking a look at yourself in the mirror. Study the shape of your face and begin drawing it on the paper. Add your features—your nose, eyes and mouth—but just in outline (fig. 1).

2. Mix one part white glue to four parts water. We will use this mixture to paint over the tissue paper, hold it, and seal it.

3. Using the scissors, or tearing the paper with your fingers, shape the pieces of tissue paper to fit your portrait. Using a brush, glue them down with the glue-and-water mixture (fig. 2).

4. Continue adding and gluing down the tissue paper, layering it where you wish the color to be darker and leaving a single layer in the areas you want lighter (fig. 3).

5. Add the background with additional tissue paper, using a solid color or pattern of your choice.

## Go Further

This tissue paper method is great for other subject matter, as well. Try making a tissue paper still life filled with fruit and flowers or one of your favorite objects.

# LAB 35 Paper Masks

## Materials

- copy paper in assorted colors
- glue stick
- scissors

### Meet the Artist: Ulla Milbrath

Artist Ulla Norup Milbrath spent a truly gypsy-like childhood traveling the world. She studied design and art history in college, and, after graduating, she created and sold art dolls and jewelry for fifteen years to clients such as the Smithsonian Museum. Find out more about Ulla at www.ullam.typepad.com.

*Festive masks* by Ulla Milbrath

**Think First:** Masks have been around since the beginning of civilization and have been used for many different purposes. The ones we are making in this Lab are for admiring on the wall, not for wearing. Many masks falling into this category show an emotion, and ours will, too! First think of the kind of emotion you want to show, and ask yourself these two things: are the eyebrows up or down, and is the mouth pulled up or down? Eyebrows that are up show surprise or happiness, depending on whether the mouth is pulled up (happy) or down (sad or surprised).

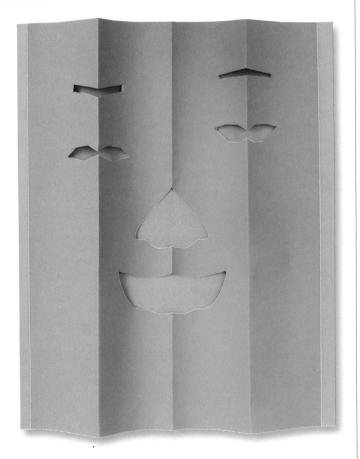

# Let's Go!

**Fig. 1:** *Fold the mask paper in half.*

**Fig. 2:** *Cut the nose out from the fold.*

1. From the colored copy paper, choose two colors that you like together or that you feel express the emotion you want to convey. Fold the one you will make the mask from in half lengthwise (fig. 1). The other paper will be used as the background.

2. Cut the nose on the fold, in the middle of the paper. Remember that it will be twice as big because you are cutting on the fold. You can make it any shape that you wish.

**Fig. 3:** *Fold in the sides.*

**Fig. 4:** *Cut out the eyes.*

3. You are now ready to cut your mask's mouth. Start at the fold and cut out one half of the mouth (fig. 2). The other side is being cut at the same time!

4. Open the paper and look at the mask, so far. Then fold each side into the middle lengthwise (fig. 3).

5. You should now have two folds. Cut one eye and one eyebrow out of each fold, above the nose (fig. 4).

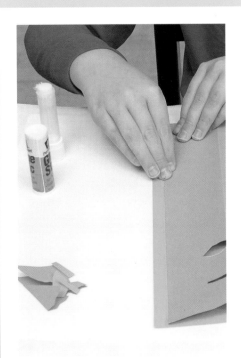

**Fig. 5:** *Glue the paper.*

6. Open the mask and line it up with the other piece of paper. Glue the sides to the back of the paper and you are done (fig. 5)!

## Go Further

Use black and white paper for a dramatic effect—no color needed!

# Torn-Paper Landscapes

Materials

- papers in assorted colors
- firm matboard for a backing
- glue stick
- scissors
- water dish
- paint brush

**Think First:** Landscapes can depict mountains, the desert, the beach, a lake, a forest, or almost anywhere on Earth! This lesson allows you to create a landscape out of your imagination. If you can't decide what to create, I recommend looking out your window or in a book for a reference. For our landscape, we imagined rolling hills on a sunny autumn day in New England.

## Go Further

Make a series of landscapes of the same place in all the different seasons.

# Let's Go!

**Fig. 1:** *For thick paper, use a paint brush and water to mark where you want to tear it.*

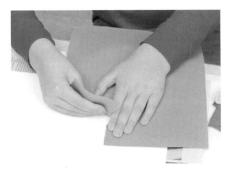

**Fig. 2:** *Tear thinner paper with your fingers guiding the way.*

1. Choose the colored papers for your landscape. We chose some hand-made papers in autumn colors.

2. To start the landscape, begin at the front of your paper, or the foreground, and work to the back, or the farthest away from you. If the paper is thick or hand-made, use a paint brush and water to mark where you want to tear it (fig. 1).

3. If your paper is not handmade or extra thick, you can just tear it slowly, with your fingers guiding the way (fig. 2).

**Fig. 3:** *Tear thick paper along the painted line of water.*

4. Continue tearing all the landscape papers to the sky (fig. 3). Create your landscape by laying out your papers on the mat board.

**Fig. 4:** *Glue the paper sky first.*

5. Beginning with the sky, glue your paper pieces onto the mat board with a glue stick, as described in Unit 1, page 25. Finish with the closest layer to the front (fig. 4).

## Meet the Artist: Molly Bosley

Molly Bosley often works with cut paper as a medium. About her work, she says, "There is a tangible presence of hands in my artwork, meaning it is very obviously handled, touched, dirtied, and stepped on. It contains the imprint of the instrument that crafted it. The process is instinctive in choosing the images but structured, layered, and designed, so the different elements harmonize to produce an artwork that is wholly nostalgic." More about Molly's work can be found at www.mollybosley.com.

*Tree House* by Molly Bosley

# Texture Monsters

- cardstock
- construction paper for background
- watercolor pans
- container of water
- paintbrush
- texture plates
- oil pastel
- pencil
- glue stick
- scissors
- newspaper and paper towels

**Think First:** Consider all the friendly monsters you have seen in books and in movies. Do they have horns or bushy hair? Perhaps they have big ears or long tails. You are the artist and you get to decide what features your monster will have. Because we will make the textured, colored papers ourselves and collage them together, you get to decide what colors your monster will be. You can sketch a few monsters out first, if you like—or not!

## Go further

Monster cards are always a welcome sight for a birthday or a get well greeting!

# Let's Go!

*Fig. 1: Add texture designs to your paper.*

*Fig. 2: Cut out the parts of the monster.*

*Fig. 3: Glue down the pieces.*

1. Choose a texture plate (or other texture-maker; see Unit 1, page 24) for your design and place your paper on top of it. Rub the oil pastel over the top of the paper to highlight the texture underneath (fig. 1).

2. Make several different texture patterns, so you will have enough papers for your entire monster. When finished, paint over the papers with a contrasting watercolor color. Let the papers dry completely.

3. Draw on the backside of the paper with a pencil to create a guideline for cutting out your monster parts.

4. Cut out the parts and assemble them on the larger paper (fig. 2).

5. Glue down the parts, as described in Unit 1, page 25 (fig. 3).

## Meet the Artist: Rebecca Emberley

Rebecca Emberley has been writing and illustrating children's books for many years. "I like to do lots of other arty things," she says. "My current interest is silkscreening; I sew, I do graphic design work, and this year I even dabbled in music production. I have lived in many places and love to travel—it keeps my perspective fresh. I like to learn how other people live." Visit www. rebeccaemberley.com for more information on Rebecca and her talented family!

*Beasties* by Rebecca Emberley

# LAB 38 Map Collage

## Materials

- old atlases or maps from travel services
- colored paper for a background support (or paint or color your own)
- glue stick for paper
- scrap paper for applying glue
- scissors
- black permanent marker
- optional: watercolors, colored pencils, markers

## Go Further

- Add details with other types of paper.
- If you don't have colored paper for the background, make your own background with details or lots of color with watercolors, markers, or crayons.

**Think First:** Open up your map if it is folded, or cut a map page from the atlas. For this project, the larger the map, the better. Maps usually have some sort of colored lines showing borders, rivers, roads, and railways. These lines can form contours of objects. Maps also have colored areas or regions, which can also form objects. Take your time looking for animals, people, buildings, and other shapes that the map outlines for you. Squinting at the map can help this process.

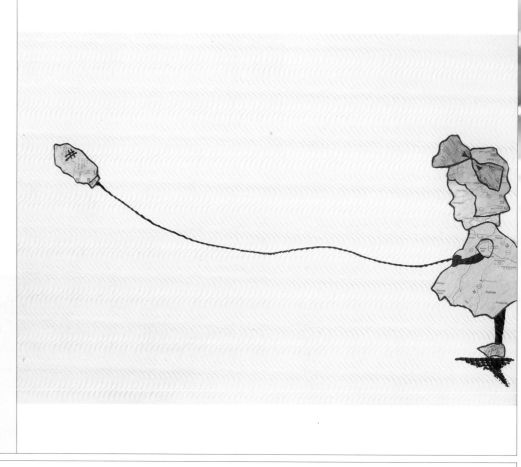

# Let's Go!

*Fig. 1:* Look for shapes in the map.

*Fig. 2:* Outline your object with black marker.

Once you are acquainted with your map, you are ready to begin.

1. Study your map again, turning it all different ways to find shapes.

2. Some maps might reveal animals or people. Others might reveal man-made objects or objects from the natural world, such as pinecones or flowers. Much depends on what you—the artist—is thinking about when you study the map (fig. 1).

*Fig. 3:* Cut out the object.

*Fig. 4:* Arrange and rearrange your pieces.

3. Once you find an object or two in your map, use the black marker to draw around the contours of your objects (fig. 2).

4. Cut out the shapes, cutting along the lines you have drawn (fig. 3).

5. Lay out the objects on your background paper, arranging them any way you choose (fig. 4). After all, you are the artist, so you know how they should go!

6. Add color to the pieces with watercolor or colored pencils, and let them dry.

7. Glue the pieces in your arrangement onto the background paper. Use the gluing method described in Unit 1, page 25. Add small details with a marker.

## Meet the Author:
## Susan Schwake

In this map collage, I found a house lurking in a map of Southern France that I bought on vacation. The piece of map inspired this small artwork called *Communication*. The background was painted with acrylic, the house was glued down, and the telephone wires, pole, and birds were painted on last. Maps inspire me!

*Communication* by Susan Schwake

# Text as Texture

- watercolor paper
- old book pages
- container of water
- tracing paper
- mirror
- pencil
- glue stick
- scissors
- optional: water-soluble colored pencils
- optional: watercolor pans and paintbrush

**Think First:** Look closely in the mirror. Which parts of yourself would you like to draw? Which parts would you like to add texture to using letters and words? You can choose your head or hair, your clothing, or the background. You can choose all of them, if you wish!

## Go Further

Use a still life for your subject and add books or newspapers to your composition for fun!

# Let's Go!

*Fig. 1: Start with a contour drawing.*

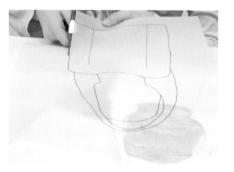

*Fig. 2: Cut the parts from the tracing paper.*

*Fig. 3: Trace the pattern on the book page.*

*Fig. 4: Glue down the pieces.*

## Meet the Artist: Larry Reynolds

Larry Reynolds is a mixed-media artist who loves to alter books, postcards, and other objects with his often humorous additions. He is active in Art Esprit, Rochester, New Hampshire's nonprofit arts group, and participates in many mail art projects.

*Larry Reynolds After Degas*
by Larry Reynolds

1. Study yourself in the mirror. With a pencil, make a contour drawing of yourself (fig. 1). Add a few major details, such as facial features and clothing.

2. Once you have your drawing done, choose the parts you want to add text to. Trace over them with the tracing paper, using a pencil.

3. Cut the parts from the tracing paper, along the traced lines (fig. 2). You now have a pattern to cut out your book pages with.

4. Place the pattern over the book pages to find the exact paper to cut out. Trace the pattern on the book page, and cut it out (fig. 3).

5. Glue down the parts, as described in Unit 1, page 25 (fig. 4).

6. If desired, use watercolors or watercolor pencils to add color to your collage.

# LAB 40 Vellum Adventures

## Materials

- Dura-Lar or thick vellum
- container of water
- paint brush
- acrylic paint
- thread, any colors
- needle with a small head
- pencil
- a plant or flower
- optional: colored pencils

**Think First:** Artist Lisa Solomon's work in our gallery has mesmerized us. She often works on transparent surfaces—with the images seemingly floating on the page. Her doily work on Dura-Lar inspired this Lab. For subject matter, find a bit of nature that you can bring into the studio to study without harming the surrounding area. (Always ask before picking anything!) For our project, we brought in some fungi from the woods. A single flower or a potted plant would also work well. Examine the object and decide how you wish to represent it in a drawing, thinking about the overall composition, as well.

## Go Further

- There are many ways to make stitches. Lisa Solomon often uses French knots in her work. Learn a few new stitches from a good embroidery book from your library. Try them out in your artwork!

- Make your paper pop up from the surface by sewing on smaller pieces of vellum or Dura-Lar that you have cut to size.

# Let's Go!

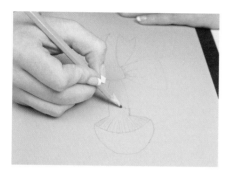

*Fig. 1: Draw your subject on the Dura-Lar.*

*Fig. 3: Add details with pencil lines.*

## Meet the Artist: Lisa Solomon

Of her work, Lisa Solomon says, "I started using vellum because I loved the texture, feel, and tone of it. I soon realized that I loved how I could work on both sides of it even more. I'm very interested in dimensionality, and the vellum allows me to play with that; it lets the viewer see both the back and the front of a work simultaneously. Plus, the needle holes I poke almost disappear, making the thread appear like magic."

*Fig. 2: Add color with paint.*

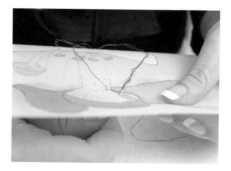

*Fig. 4: Stitch along the pencil lines.*

1. Begin by drawing the object you have chosen as your subject matter with a pencil on the Dura-Lar. It can be set in a natural setting or a fantasy setting, as we have shown here (fig. 1).

2. When the drawing is done, decide which parts to paint with color (fig. 2), which to add colored pencil to, and which parts you'd like to stitch.

3. When painting on vellum or Dura-Lar, be sure your brush only contains a thick paint and no water. Water can create wrinkles in these types of paper.

4. Add more details or outlines with colored pencil or regular pencil, if desired (fig. 3).

5. Thread the needle and tie a knot in the end of the thread. Start at the back of the paper and stitch along the pencil lines, completing your artwork (fig. 4)!

*Doily No. 24 by Lisa Solomon*

# Make Your Own Collage Papers

## Materials

- white cardstock
- watercolor pans
- soft paint brush
- container of water
- drinking straw
- shallow container for bubble printing
- liquid dish soap
- liquid acrylic paint
- old credit card
- newspaper and paper towels

**Think First:** This Lab is designed to create beautiful papers to use with other Labs. You can print on them, cut them up to use in collages, paint black ink on them, or make greeting cards, gift tags, and bookmarks from them. The possibilities are endless. Having a nice supply of hand-textured papers in the studio is always a good idea. The bonus of making your own is that you are doing just that: making. This Lab can really jump-start your creative process!

### Go Further

Experiment with other methods of painting. We taped four paint brushes together and painted with them simultaneously!

# Let's Go!

*Fig. 1:* *Tap with one finger.*

*Fig. 2:* *Blow beads of paint with a straw.*

*Fig. 3:* *Blow low in the container and slowly to avoid splurts!*

*Fig. 4:* *Acrylic smear painting*

1. Set up your painting area as described in Unit 1, page 20. We will begin with spatter painting. Load your brush with lots of water, then stroke the watercolor pan to get the color onto your brush.

2. Hold the brush over the paper and tap it with one finger from your other hand (fig. 1). This is called indoor spatter painting. No wrist or full arm fling required!

3. Now we will try straw painting. Load up your brush as in Step 1, but this time make small beads of watery paint all over the paper.

4. Place your straw very close to a bead and blow (fig. 2). Turn your paper to direct the movement of the bead. Remember to stop and take a few breaths in between bursts of air.

5. Bubble painting requires your straw again. In the shallow container, mix one part liquid paint to four parts water. Add half a part liquid dish soap. Blow low and slow through your straw into the container to make a bubble mountain (fig. 3).

6. Roll your paper over the top to print your bubbles!

7. Acrylic smear painting is fun and dramatic. Drip a few drops of liquid acrylic paint on the paper. Use an old credit card or similar tool to wipe the paint around the paper. Cover all of the paper with color (fig. 4).

## Meet the Artist: Beth Olshansky

Beth Olshansky is the director of the Center for the Advancement of Art-Based Literacy at the University of New Hampshire. She is the developer of two art-based literacy models: Picturing Writing: Fostering Literacy through Art, and Image-Making Within the Writing Process.

A collage made with hand-painted papers by Beth Olshansky

# 42 Pop Art Collage

Materials

- tracing paper
- colored paper
- pencil
- glue stick
- scissors
- any canned goods, from cleaning to food products

**Think First:** Find a product that appeals to you, either in color or in the design of the label. Something with a bold graphic look is fun. You will repeat the image a number of times, so when choosing, think of your object in multiples, as on a grocery store shelf.

## Go Further

Make a trip to a museum or library to view some of Andy Warhol's soup cans. Try making a collage with a dozen images of your favorite soup!

# Let's Go!

*Fig. 1:* Cut out the patterns.

*Fig. 2:* Trace around the patterns.

1. Begin by drawing the image on the tracing paper. Keep the areas of the image simple, so you can separate them by color.
2. Decide which parts of the image you want to cut from the colored papers. For example, we chose the lid, the rim, the coffee cup, the shadow, and the rest of the can. Cut them from your drawing into separate pattern pieces (fig. 1).

*Fig. 3:* Glue the pieces down.

3. Use a pencil to trace the patterns onto the colored paper (fig. 2), and then cut out the pieces. We will make two of our coffee cans, so we will need two of each piece to make them. You can make two or twenty of the same objects—it's your choice!

## Meet the Artist: Erik Boettcher

Erik Boettcher works with paper and mixed media in his artwork. He creates many pop iconic works featuring amusement rides, sports cars, roadside attractions, and holiday destinations from the '60s. His work is held in private collections around the world. He lives and works in New Hampshire.

*Skee Ball* by Erik Boettcher

*Fig. 4:* Draw in small details with a marker.

4. Glue the pieces onto the background paper (fig. 3).
5. If desired, add details with a permanent marker (fig. 4).

# Mixed Media

**THE DARLING OF THE POPULAR ART WORLD** for the past few years has been mixed media. It is no stranger to fine art, with Picasso and Braque leading the way, their first collage paintings hosting bits of lowly newsprint glued down amid the oil paint. The Labs in this Unit will inspire students to look for a second or third medium to complete a challenge in their work. Sometimes that means drawing with glue and adding color with magazine clippings. Other times the medium becomes the "drawn" line or subject matter itself. Mixed media is fun right from the start, and these Labs will produce different results each time they are used.

UNIT

6

## Materials

- canvas or board
- pencil
- acrylic paint
- acrylic medium
- paintbrush
- scissors
- palette
- newspaper
- assortment of papers
- easel

### Go Further

Be inspired by a special ticket stub you find in your coat pocket, a letter you received in the mail, or even junk mail. Cut it up and create a mixed-media artwork based on the paper you are including!

**Think First:** This painting relies on paint and paper to complement your subject matter. We chose to paint a small sculpture, made by the student. You can choose any subject. Examine your subject and decide which parts of the composition you would like to enhance with paper.

# Let's Go!

Fig. 1: Sketch lightly on your canvas.

Fig. 2: Cut and place the paper inclusions.

1. Begin with a light sketch on your canvas (fig. 1).

2. Decide which parts of your artwork will have paper. Experiment with your composition by cutting those parts from the papers and placing them on the canvas (fig. 2).

3. When you are satisfied with the arrangement, set up the acrylic paint, as described in Unit 1, page 20 and paint your canvas, being mindful of the brush strokes you wish to have and the

Fig. 3: Paint your canvas first.

variety of values in your color. Use an easel to work with the paint (fig. 3).

4. When the paint is dry, put your canvas flat on the table. Brush a little acrylic medium onto the back of your paper pieces and press them onto the canvas. Brush over the pieces with more medium to secure (fig. 4).

5. Continue with all the pieces, until finished. Coat the artwork with another layer of medium to seal it (fig. 5).

## Meet the Artist:
## Mati Rose McDonough

Mati Rose McDonough is an adult who paints like a child. It has taken her thirty-two years, two schools, and approximately 486 paintings to get to this point. Find out more about Mati Rose at www.matirose.com.

*Red Elephant* by Mati Rose McDonough

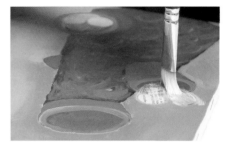

Fig. 4: Glue the paper with acrylic medium.

Fig. 5: Coat the entire artwork to finish.

# Charcoal and Watercolor

- 90-lb. watercolor paper
- vine charcoal
- watercolor pans
- soft watercolor brushes
- a landscape photograph from a magazine or a photograph of a favorite place

**Think First:** Study the photograph of your landscape. Think about which parts of the photo to include in your composition. Decide what time of day it is in the photo and how that affects the colors in the photo.

## Go Further

- Try an imaginary landscape instead of a real one.
- Use this mixed-media method to make a portrait of your favorite person!

# Let's Go!

**Fig. 1:** *Draw in the landscape from back to front.*

**Fig. 2:** *Fill in the details.*

**Fig. 3:** *Add color with watercolor paint.*

**Fig. 4:** *Paint over the charcoal for a softened effect.*

## Meet the Author: Susan Schwake

"I often use charcoal with watercolor, because I love the contrast that charcoal can give. In this imaginary landscape, I have used a sharp piece of vine charcoal to create the black tones in this painting—the seaweed and the birds."

*Three by the Sea* by Susan Schwake

1. With the charcoal, lightly draw the horizon line and the elements of the background on the watercolor paper.

2. Continue working forward, adding the middle ground and finally the foreground (fig. 1).

3. Keeping the charcoal light, add any landscape details you want to include (fig. 2).

4. When you have all of the elements of the landscape drawn, you are ready for paint. Using the watercolor, begin to paint (fig. 3). Focus on showing where the light is coming from, the time of day, and the season.

5. For a crisp line, work the paint up to the charcoal line; for a softened effect, gently paint over the charcoal (fig. 4).

# Acrylic and Ink Abstracts

- canvas board or stretched canvas (any size)
- India ink
- acrylic paint
- soft and bristle brushes
- Plexiglas palette
- palette knife
- drinking straw

**Think First:** Set up your workspace with a palette for acrylic paint, as described in Unit 1, page 20. Experiment with blowing one or two drops of ink across the paper with the straw. Keep the end of the straw close to, but not touching, the ink for best results. Turn the paper as you blow to direct the ink. Make sure to breathe normally between blows through the straw, or you might get dizzy!

Think about where you would like to place your first three dots of ink. Remember what happened when you did your test blows on the paper. Think beyond the first three, if you want to plan it out, or just go with the three and see what happens. Experimentation is a big part of art, and sometimes just going with the process is the best method. This exercise is part chance, part creativity, and all fun. It is all about finding images hidden in the ink splotches (or not!) then having fun pulling out all the stops with the paint.

## Meet the Artist: Jen Garrido

Jen Garrido's artwork inspired this Lab and the negative-space drawing Lab (Lab 8). Of her work, Jen says, "I construct my paintings and drawings using a delicate balance of choice and process." You can see more of Jen's work at www.jenngarrido.com.

*Windy but Holding* by Jen Garrido

# Let's Go!

*Fig. 1:* Use slow breaths of air to control the ink flow. Short bursts of air will make the ink spray in all directions.

1. Drop the first three ink droplets onto your canvas and blow them around until you are satisfied with the results (fig. 1).

2. Turn and examine the canvas to see if you have any emerging images. Make decisions about where to put more drops based on what you see (fig. 2).

3. Continue in groups of three drops at a time, until you are happy with the amount of ink and shapes you have on your canvas. Make sure some of your ink lines cross each other to make new shapes.

4. Let the ink dry completely while you dispense the acrylic paint on the palette, as described in Unit 1, page 20.

5. Looking at your ink blotches will tell you a lot about what colors to choose. You might end up with a face, a giraffe, a landscape, or a completely abstract design. Choose your colors to bring out the most important lines and shapes in your artwork (fig. 3).

*Fig. 2:* Additional drops are added after looking carefully at the work, so far.

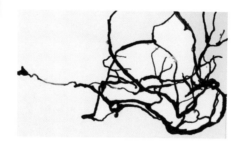

*Fig. 3:* What do you see in your image? What colors are you going to choose to finish it?

6. Follow the instructions in Unit 1 for working with acrylic paint. Use red, yellow, blue, and white to mix new colors on your palette with the palette knife (fig. 4).

7. Continue painting until you have filled in all the spaces between the ink blotches. Apply a second layer if

*Fig. 4:* Use a palette knife to mix colors.

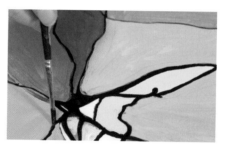

*Fig. 5:* Repaint your black ink lines to make them stand out again.

the paint seems too thin in places. Sometimes this happens with yellows and other light colors.

8. If any of the black lines have become painted over, go over them with the soft brush and ink. This will keep the lines of your images crisp (fig. 5).

## Go Further

Try limiting your color choices to two colors, or use just one with the addition of white to make a range of values.

# Paper Family Quilts

Materials

- large sheet of heavyweight drawing paper
- pencil
- watercolor pans
- paintbrush
- oil pastels
- container of water
- newspaper
- paper towels

**Think First:** Artist Faith Ringgold's work, plus our own fond memories of our family, will inspire us in this Lab. Quilts can be a way of documenting life stories. Think of things you like to do with your family. Where do you do them? Do you go on special trips or adventures? Each square, or quilt block, we design will represent one of those memories.

## Go Further

Your paper quilt can incorporate more than drawing and painting. Find bits of ribbon, lace, or special papers to glue on. Faith Ringgold sewed fabric borders around her paintings—you can too!

# Let's Go!

**Fig. 1:** *Draw your family.*

**Fig. 2:** *Draw with oil pastels.*

**Fig. 3:** *Draw in stitches and details.*

**Fig. 4:** *Paint in each square.*

1. Begin by creating a large square in the center of your paper. This will be the focal point for your paper quilt. Sketch in your family (fig. 1).

2. Using a ruler, draw lines radiating out of the corners of the center drawing. These spaces are for your memory blocks.

3. Continue with a pencil, then switch to oil pastels to draw in the large family block and the outer memory blocks (fig. 2).

4. Leave spaces around your drawing for adding the watercolors. Make little fancy stitches around the lines between the blocks, just like a fabric quilt would have (fig. 3).

5. To finish the quilt, paint each square to cover all remaining white paper areas (fig. 4). You can select a specific palette of colors or use them all!

## Meet the Artist: Faith Ringgold

Faith Ringgold is an American artist, who grew up in Harlem in New York City. She earned her masters degree in painting and traveled to Europe to study the masters. Her beautiful paintings, story quilts, and sculptures express the memories and movements of African Americans during the '60s and beyond. Ringgold says, "If one can, anyone can. All you gotta do is try." When my children were young, we read *Tar Beach*. It inspired this lesson. See Ringgold's work in a museum or gallery, or visit her website: www.faithringgold.com.

# Watercolor and Pencil

- watercolor paper
- pencil
- watercolor pans
- paintbrush
- colored pencils
- container of water
- newspaper
- paper towels

**Think First:** Using a variety of media to create an artwork can be a very natural process. In this Lab, we use a reference model (a book about birds) to create a imaginary animal based on features of a real one. Think about the parts of your artwork you would like to do in paint and which you would like to do in pencil. You can alternate between materials to get your desired results!

## Go Further

Make a portrait, including a person or flowers, like our featured artist, Flossy-P, has!

# Let's Go!

Fig. 1: *Paint color into the drawing.*

Fig. 2: *Draw with colored pencils.*

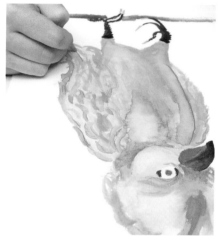

Fig. 3: *Draw in details.*

1. Find your reference material and begin your graphite pencil drawing on the paper.

2. Add color with the watercolor first (fig. 1). Remember that wet next to wet will run—which sometimes can be a good thing!

3. Continue with colored pencils for line definition or to add pattern (fig. 2).

4. Add small details with the pencils (fig. 3).

## Meet the Artist: Flossy-P

Flossy-P lives in a small coastal village in Australia with her husband and new little baby boy. She says the ideas for her work come from seeing and becoming captured by things or moments or people that others usually wouldn't even notice. More of her delightful illustrations and artwork (and the story behind her name!) can be found at www.flossyparticles.com.

*Curiosity* by Flossy-P

# Photos in My Painting

- canvas board or primed Masonite board
- container of water
- newspaper
- acrylic paint
- Plexiglas palette
- water decal paper
- bristle brushes
- soft brushes
- acrylic medium
- digital photo

**Think First:** Find a digital photo of yourself or someone you know to inspire this artwork. Using the water decal paper (see Resources, page 140), print out your image in black and white. Cut it to the edge of the image and place it on your blank canvas. Think about what the person is feeling, where he or she is, or what mood he or she conveys. Decide how you want to express this in your work: with color, symbols, lines, or composition.

## Go Further

- You can use copyright-free images to create all sorts of artwork this way. The decals are a simple method of transferring images to your work.

- Try using a historical photo, like our featured artist Susanna Gordon did!

# Let's Go!

*Fig. 1: Begin painting the background.*

*Fig. 2: Put the decal in the water and remove the backing.*

1. Begin with the background. Paint the colors and shapes without detail (fig. 1).

2. Put your decal in the water for about one minute. It will start to slip off the backing (fig. 2).

3. When the paint is dry, place the decal on the background layer of your painting and smooth it out with your fingertips. Let dry completely (fig. 3).

*Fig. 3: Apply the decal.*

4. Paint a layer of acrylic medium over the decal and into the painting (fig. 4).

5. Continue painting, incorporating the decal into your work (fig. 5).

## Meet the Artist: Susanna Gordon

Susanna is a Canadian currently living in the United States. Encaustic painting is part of Susanna's intriguing work, which sometimes includes her own beautiful photography. See more of her work at www.susannassketch book.typepad.com.

*Fig. 4: Paint a layer of acrylic medium over your work.*

*Fig. 5: Add more detail with paint.*

*To the Farmhouse by Susanna Gordon*

# Larger-Than-Life Portraits

- large piece of heavyweight cardstock or poster paper
- pencil
- mirror
- old magazines
- scissors
- glue stick

**Think First:** Using a mirror, study yourself and note the shapes you find in your face, hair, and features. We will simplify them all, so think in large shapes. You can use a photograph, if you prefer, but I encourage you to use a mirror and work from life as much as you possibly can. If you use a digital photograph, you can use a photo editing program to simplify the image and give yourself a head start on the shapes. But working from life always teaches you the most! This Lab was inspired by art teacher extraordinaire, Karen Good.

## Go Further

Try a pet portrait or your favorite zoo animal for this Lab!

# Let's Go!

*Fig. 1:* Sketch yourself on paper.

*Fig. 2:* Cut out and sort the colored papers.

*Fig. 3:* Arrange your shapes on your pencil drawing.

*Fig. 4:* Glue down the colorful cut papers.

1. Make a light sketch of yourself, using large shapes and not too much detail (fig. 1).

2. Open your magazines and cut shapes from the pages that include the range of colors to represent your skin tones, hair, clothing, and eyes (fig. 2). You can cut out text, too, if you want to add that!

3. Arrange the shapes on your pencil drawing (fig. 3). For the best effect, use a wide range of values.

4. Using a glue stick and the gluing methods described in Unit 1, glue your papers onto the paper (fig. 4).

5. Work to the edges, to fill your collage completely. Use a permanent marker for tiny details, if you like!

## Meet the Artist: Amber Lavalley

Amber Lavalley is an artist and art educator from New Hampshire. Her works are often portraits—both self-portraits and portraits of others. She has won awards for her painting and continues to explore mixed media, as well as more traditional oils, in her work. Amber teaches with me at artstream studios, and we are honored to often have her work on display.

*Light Sleep* by Amber Lavalley

# Batik Landscapes

- washed and ironed white woven cotton fabric
- pencil
- liquid acrylics
- small containers for paint
- clear glue
- masking tape
- newspaper
- wax paper
- water containers
- dishpan
- Plexiglas

**Think First:** Batik is an ancient art form that uses wax to block out colored dye in patterns. The blocking process leaves a white line where the wax was. We are going to use clear glue for this process, instead of hot wax, and liquid acrylic paints, instead of dyes. Think about a simple landscape that you would like to make. Is there a lot of sky and a little land? What time of day or season is it? What is the weather like? Answering these questions will help you determine your composition.

## Go Further

Use your batik fabric to make a cushion or a wall hanging.

# Let's Go!

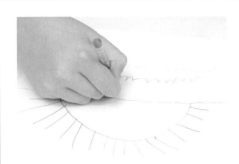

*Fig. 1:* Sketch your composition on paper.

*Fig. 2:* Apply the glue.

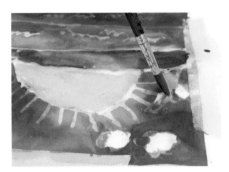

*Fig. 3:* Paint with liquid acrylic.

*Fig. 4:* Wash out the glue.

1. Sketch out your ideas first on paper with pencil (fig. 1).

2. Tape your fabric over wax paper attached to a firm backing, such as your Plexiglas plate.

3. Start drawing with the glue. Make sure you have a solid line of glue, so it blocks out the fabric from the paint. Let dry completely (fig. 2).

4. Paint the areas with the liquid acrylic paint. Don't scrub the brush too much over the glue. Let it dry overnight (fig. 3).

5. Wash out the glue with a little liquid soap and warm water. Scrub lightly with your fingers to get the glue out. Let dry and iron (fig. 4).

## Meet the Artist: Batik by Nancy

Batik by Nancy is a little company from Brooklyn, New York. The owners, Tammy and Nancy, are a mother/daughter team who have created colorful batik clothing and accessories since the 1970s in their shop on Atlantic Avenue. Their work has been worn on television by the Cosby Show kids and by thousands of people all over the world. Each and every one of their pieces is made by hand. Visit them at 492 Atlantic Avenue, Brooklyn, New York, or online at www.nancybatik.com.

*The Cow Jumped Over the Moon* by Batik by Nancy

# Contact Paper Insects

- wooden panel
- contact paper (any pattern)
- black permanent marker
- watercolor pencils
- soft brushes
- scissors
- optional: watercolor paints

**Think First:** For this Lab, we will use patterned contact paper for the subject matter. Try bright patterns, faux wood, and stone—any kind will do. The idea is to use out-of-the-ordinary art materials for a mixed-media work. Decide on the insects that you would like to create using a book or photographs of them as references. Think, too, of where your insects would like to live (the setting in which they will be shown), and sketch out the idea, if you want to, first.

## Go Further

Make a whole flower garden from contact paper using different patterns of paper. Add insects to the flowers.

# Let's Go!

**Fig. 1:** *Cut out insects from the contact paper.*

**Fig. 2:** *Add detail with black marker.*

1. Using your black marker, draw your insect shapes on the back of the contact paper. Cut them out with scissors (fig. 1).

2. Add details with black permanent marker on top of the contact paper (fig. 2).

3. Lay the insects out on your wooden panel (fig. 3). Arrange them as you would like them to be—we will stick them on later.

**Fig. 3:** *Decide where the insects will go.*

4. Color your background with the watercolor pencils or watercolor paints (fig. 4).

5. Using your water and soft brush, soften the watercolor pencil lines.

6. Let the work dry completely. Peel the backing from the insects and stick them onto the wood panel (fig. 5).

## Meet the Artist: Camilla Stacey

Camilla Stacey is an artist from the United Kingdom who works in a wide variety of media—from lusterware figurines to printmaking, as well as textile brooches and vintage remixes. The print shown—which inspired this Lab!—is on Fablon sticky back plastic. See more of Camilla's work at: http://madebymilla.blogspot.com and also at http://curatorialpracticelog.blogspot.com.

**Fig. 4:** *Draw in the colored pencil backgrounds.*

**Fig. 5:** *Peel and stick the insects on the artwork.*

*Chickadee on Fablon* by Camilla Stacey

## Materials

- small wooden panel
- tacky glue
- glue stick for paper
- papers with plant inclusions
- scissors
- assortment of natural found objects

**Think First:** Take a walk outside in a park or the woods. Look for leaves, bark, seed pods, or other fallen (don't pick!) flora on the ground. Flat pieces are best, but you can glue most anything to your panel. We chose some fallen birch bark to use. You don't need much to get started. Think about your composition and how it relates to your little collection from your walk.

### Go Further

Make your collection into pictures, without gluing them down—and take a photo of them. You can rearrange the same nature bits into different photos.

# Let's Go!

***Fig. 1:*** *Cut the trees from the birch bark.*

***Fig. 2:*** *Arrange the collage.*

***Fig. 3:*** *Glue down all of the pieces.*

1. Based on the collection of items you found, decide on your composition. Because we found birch bark, we chose to cut trees from the bark (fig. 1).

2. Look for other elements to add to your nature collage. We chose papers with bits of leaves and grass for backgrounds.

3. Cut your pieces of paper and arrange the items as you want to glue them down until you are satisfied with the composition (fig. 2).

4. Starting from the back, glue all the elements down, using the paper glue stick for the paper and tacky glue for the heavier elements (fig. 3).

## Meet the Artist: Amanda Woodward

Amanda Woodward is a Canadian designer, illustrator, and artist. She heads her own design studio, Woodward Design, in Edmonton, Alberta. Although she has worked on everything from ad campaigns to visual identities, her passion for illustration often touches her work. Her illustration client list includes Alberta Milk; *Cricket* magazine, Scholastic, and Target, among others. This Lab was inspired by a birch bark mobile that Amanda made and then turned into this beautiful illustration. See more of Amanda's paintings at www.amandawoodward.com.

*Birch mobile* by Amanda Woodward

# Resources

## Australia

**Eckersley's Arts, Crafts, and Imagination**

www.eckersleys.com.au

## Canada

**Curry's Art Store**

Ontario, Canada

www.Currys.com

art and craft supplies

**DeSerres**

www.deserres.ca

**Michaels**

www.michaels.com

**Opus Framing & Art Supplies**

www.opusframing.com

## France

**Graphigro**

Paris, France

www.graphigro.com

## Italy

**Vertecchi**

Rome, Italy

www.vertecchi.com

## New Zealand

**Littlejohns Art & Graphic Supplies Ltd.**

Wellington, New Zealand

PH 04 385 2099

FAX 04 385 2090

## United Kingdom

**T N Lawrence & Son Ltd.**

www.lawrence.co.uk

**Creative Crafts**

www.creativecrafts.co.uk

**HobbyCraft Group Limited**

www.hobbycraft.co.uk

## United States

**A. C. Moore**

www.acmoore.com

**Ampersand Art Supply**

www.ampersandart.com

**Dick Blick**

www.dickblick.com

**DecalPaper.com**

www.decalpaper.com

**Golden Artist Colors**

www.goldenpaints.com

**Hobby Lobby**

www.hobbylobby.com

**Homasote Board**

www.homasote.com

**Jo-Ann Fabric and Craft Stores**

www.joann.com

**Michaels**

www.michaels.com

**Preval Sprayer**

www.preval.com

**Pro Chemical and Dye**

www.prochemicalanddye.com

**Daniel Smith**

www.danielsmith.com

**Utrecht**

www.utrechtart.com

**The Art Lab Kids:** Alicia, Alyson, Bella, Caanan, Chloe, Daria, Eilideh, Emily, Grace, Haiden, Ilona, Izabella, Jayden, Joseph, Kaleb, Kate, Keegan, Keith, Kelsey, Lauren, Liam, Maeve, Miles, Morgan, Robby, Robi, Skye, and Susan

# Contributing Artists

**Daisy Adams**, 53
www.etsy.com/shop/DaisyAdamsArtwork

**Sally Allen**, 47
www.gentlejourney.net

**Darryl Joel Berger**, 55, 67
www.Red-handed.blogspot.com

**Joe Blajda**, 37
Manchester, NH, USA

**Erik Boettcher**, 117
Dover, NH, USA

**Megan Bogonovich**, 77
www.meganbogonovich.com

**Molly Bosley**, 105
www.mollybosley.com

**Judith Heller Cassell**, 87
Rochester, NH, USA

**Nancy Cogen and Tamara Johnson**, 135
www.nancybatik.com

**Lisa Congdon**, 65
www.lisacongdon.com

**John Terry Downs**, 89
Plymouth State University
New Hampshire, USA

**Rebecca Emberley**, 107
www.rebeccaemberley.com

**Edibeth Farrington**, 83
New Hampshire, USA

**Flossy-P**, 129
www.flossyparticles.com
Australia

**Jen Garrido**, 42, 124
www.jengarrido.com

**Susanna Gordon**, 131
www.susannassketchbook.typepad.com

**Noelle Griskey**, 97
www.pinkbathtub.com

**Amber Lavalley**, 133
www.artstreamstudios.com/shop

# About the Author

Susan Schwake is an artist, art educator, and curator. She actively exhibits her own work in galleries around the United States and Europe and sells her work online and in her own gallery, artstream. Susan has been part of juried public art exhibitions, creating large-scale, site-specific works.

Her passion for teaching and making art with others grew from a tiny seed of an idea in the fourth grade. Working in such diverse settings as schools, community centers, special needs nonprofits, summer camps, intergenerational facilities, libraries, and her own little art school, Susan has taught art to hundreds of people over the past twenty years.

She created a permanent exhibition of children's art, involving more than 100 local children, that graces the walls of a new children's room in her local library in 1997 and refreshed it in 2007 on the tenth anniversary. In 2000, she directed a similar project with 400 people in an intergenerational setting for a new multi-agency facility, bringing the staff, families, and clients more closely together through the process of making art. She has enjoyed many residencies in public and private schools, with whole school projects, and in special needs groups and single classrooms.

In 2005, Susan began a blog called artesprit. Through the blog, she embraced writing and photographing her world, meeting many new artists and friends around the globe.

She co-owns and is the curator for artstream in Rochester, New Hampshire. She enjoys bringing compelling group shows of contemporary art to New Hampshire. She is happy to be working alongside her husband every day doing what she loves most.

Blog: www.artesprit.blogspot.com

Website: www.susanschwake.com

Gallery: www.artstreamstudios.com

# Acknowledgments

To everyone at Quarry Books who helped make this dream possible.

To Mary Ann Hall and Betsy Gammons for their guidance, patience, and encouragement. Thank you!

To my husband, Rainer Schwake, for his beautifully quiet way of helping and his endless support for me since the day we met. (I also am eternally grateful for his sweet photography skills.)

To my daughter, Chloe, who was tireless in her help with the lessons by making art spontaneously—and beautifully.

To my daughter, Grace, who nurtured the writing process.

To my intern, Bella, who was simply amazing.

To the parents of my students, for encouraging their journey in art.

To my students, who are deep inspiration for these lessons.

. . . and to all the kids who made art for this book—they rock!